Four

Elder Carrell K. Cargle, Sr.
Presiding Elder Emeritus
Christian Methodist Episcopal Church

Tish, you are a wonderful person and may God bless you and your family with peace, love and prayer

Rev Carrell K Cargle

2/12/23

219 980 1460

Cell 773 454 6903

Four Pillars of Society

Wealth Builders Publishing House

All rights reserved. No part of this publication may be reproduced, stored in a special system, or transmitted, in any form or by any means, electronic, mechanical, photocopying, recording, or otherwise without prior permission of the publisher. This publication contains the opinions and ideas of its author and is designed to provide useful advice regarding the subject matter covered. The author and publisher specifically disclaim any responsibility for liability, loss or risk, personal or otherwise, that is incurred therefore, directly or indirectly, of the use and application of any of the contents of this book.

"Four Pillars of Society"
By:
Elder Carrell K. Cargle, Sr.
Presiding Elder Emeritus
Christian Methodist Episcopal Church

Published by Wealth Builders Publishing House.
For information write to Carla Cargle,
14090 Southwest Freeway, Ste. 300, Sugar Land, TX 77478.
(832) 291-2488 or support@wbphbooks.com

Registered Copyright © 2019 of Carrell K. Cargle, Sr.
All rights reserved.
Website: www.wbphbooks.com

Four Pillars of Society
Edited, Layout, and Book Design by Denise Bates. MSIMC

PRINTED IN THE UNITED STATES OF AMERICA

Four Pillars of Society

DEDICATION

In Honor of Mrs. Belva June "Jean" Cargle

This book is dedicated in remembrance to my dear and devoted wife, Belva June "Jean" Cargle. The one who truly showed me, "I can do all things through Christ who strengthens me." (Philippians 4:13)

When I first shared with my wife that I wanted to tell a story about creating a Christ focused partnership between Family, School, Church, and the Community, she enthusiastically gave me her support. Belva encouraged me for many years to write a book because she saw in me my dedication as a husband, father, pastor, presiding elder and a person committed to reaching the lives of people from all walks of life.

I am grateful for the years that we spent together doing God's work within the Family, the School, the Church and the Community. I thank her for serving as First Lady with grace dignity and beauty at Holsey Temple C.M.E. Church in St. Joseph, MO, Phillips Chapel C.M.E. Church in Springfield, OH, Israel Metropolitan C.M.E. Church in Gary, IN, J Claude Allen C.M.E. Church in Dixmoor, IL and First Lady of Gary and Chicago Districts of the C.M.E. Churches.

Her love and support are evident throughout this book as she labored many hours reading and digesting the hundreds of handwritten and typewritten pages in the earlier framing of my thoughts that now make up this book.

My dearest Belva died unexpectedly on Tuesday, February 21, 2017 on the "Battlefield;" doing what she dearly loved – teaching children. This book would have been impossible without her love, support and direction on this project and all of my efforts over the years. Although she has gone on to be with the Lord, I know her presence will always be with me. I find solace and comfort in knowing that she was my devoted wife, a wonderful educator and the mother of my three adult children: Carrell Jr., Derrick and Carla.

Four Pillars of Society

Table of Contents

Foreword	5
Words of Support – Ret. Bishop Paul Stewart, Sr.	6
Preface – Bishop Sylvester Williams, Sr.	7
Introduction - Bishop Henry M. Williamson, Sr.	9
PILLAR I: The Family	11
Family Workshops	57
PILLAR II: The School	71
PILLAR III: The Church	93
Spiritual Leadership Workshop	138
PILLAR IV: The Community	149
Acknowledgements	215
Appendix	219
References	229

Four Pillars of Society

FOREWORD

The author recognizes there are many institutions in the world but clearly not every institution is designed to develop and promote family. It is also the author's opinion there are only four basic institutions designed to do so. These four basic but essential institutions are: Family, School, Church and Community.

1. The **Family** is the first school the child will attend and within the context of the home the child learns his/her ABCs, communication and interpersonal relationship skill, and overall position and responsibilities.

2. The **School** is the academic foundation where educational systems and theories may be developed and mastered. The school enhances the students' ability to achieve and develop skills for an enriched capacity.

3. The **Church** is the Lord's House where people from all walks of life experiences gather and learn the teachings of God and our Lord Jesus Christ. The controlling purpose of the Church is to make Disciples of all nationalities, baptizing them in the Name of the Father, and of the Son, and of the Holy Ghost. Through the Church we learn to share the world.

4. The **Community** is defined as all of the people living in a particular section, district, and various neighborhoods sharing a common interest. Communities working together to form a union of families, schools, and churches create a sense of extended family within the context of community.

Each of these institutions, when operating with purpose and balance forms and informs morality, develops character, infuses concepts of respect for self and others and creates responsible citizens for the world.

Elder Carrell K. Cargle, Sr.

Four Pillars of Society

Words of Support

From Retired Bishop Paul A. G. Stewart, Sr.:

My experiences of working with Presiding Elder Carrell K. Cargle, Sr. as his Presiding Bishop

While I have known Presiding Elder Carrell K. Cargle, Sr. for over thirty years, it was my distinct honor and pleasure to work with him as his Presiding Bishop. While he demonstrated and possessed many admirable qualities, I will list some of them in the following statements:

I found Rev. Cargle to be a genuine, kind, friendly and loving person. He was an outstanding model of a loving and faithful husband and a generous and caring father. There no doubts that he was committed to his family and God.

In his work as a pastor and Presiding Elder, Rev. Cargle sponsored and coordinated more training sessions for local preachers and ministers on trial than any other presiding Elder than I have known. He was very efficient, honest, accountable and compassionate in all of his activities. He exemplified an unusual love and passion for the C.M.E. Church in particular, and the universal church in general.

I would like to summarize my experiences of working with Rev, Cargle, by stating that he served as an outstanding Christian shepherd. He was a shepherd who cared for, protected and effectively led both clergy and laity to become better Christians and servants of God.

Four Pillars of Society

PREFACE

Over the years the observant and astute mind has witnessed a drastic change in our nation and indeed our global society. Many have said 'things aren't the way they used to be," in reference to the decline in morality, increase in violence, disregard for others, etc. According to Reverend Carrell K. Cargle, Sr., former Pastor and present Presiding Elder Emeritus in the CME Church, our society is a reflection and result of the institutions that shape us. Having grown up in a Christian home coupled with his biblical scholarship and years of pastoral experience, Presiding Elder Emeritus Cargle, outlines four pillars of our society, that not only positively nurtured him but will also nurture and shape future generations to become a society of peace and harmony.

The first pillar he describes is the home and family. It is the home that initially teaches Godly principles, and developmental concepts of love, respect, responsibility, obedience, discipline, etc. Indeed, for many of us, how we acted away from home was a reflection of how we had learned these concepts at home. Some of us even remember our parents saying the way we acted publicly was a reflection of our home training.

Another pillar is the school that not only taught the three r's, (reading, 'riting,' and 'rithmetic'), but further instilled home values and religious principles. Historically, especially in rural area, religious devotional services started the school day thereby reinforcing the Godly principles initially learned in the home.

In addition to the home and school, needless to say, the church further instilled values and morals. The church and school have seemingly always worked together in that many churches provided a place of worship on Sundays, but

Four Pillars of Society

converted to schools and educational facilities through the week. Additionally, churches sponsored and financed institutions of higher education, thereby, continuing to promote morals and values that promote positive citizenship and a responsible society.

Lastly, the community cultivated shared values between its citizens. Many persons now recall being taught, chastised, and disciplined by several seniors in the community often for the same undesirable behavior. If one misbehaved publicly, not only were there immediate consequences from the elders of the community, but later, consequences at home. Indeed, the understanding was "it takes a village to raise a child."

Although the initial place of learning morals and values is the home, Reverend Cargle credits the school, church and community as important pillars of learning as well. His book is a "must read" for all who recognize the importance of the aforementioned institutions for shaping a harmonious and peaceful society.

Bishop Sylvester Williams, Sr.

Four Pillars of Society

INTRODUCTION

"Let the elders that rule well be counted worthy of double honour, especially they who labour in the word and doctrine." I Timothy 5:17 *(KJV)*

I am happy to encourage all members in the Christian Methodist Episcopal Church to both read and study the book by Dr. Carrell K. Cargle, Sr., Presiding Elder emeritus both of Gary and Chicago Districts. I came to know him more than 50 years ago when he served as my pastor of the Israel CME Church of Gary, Indiana. He became an excellent spiritual father and encourager in my youth and later as a spiritual father when I accepted my Call to Ministry at 17 years of age. He along with Bishop J. Claude Allen helped shape and direct my focus as a young adult preacher and later as pastor at 19 years of age at the Westside CME Church in Gary. He has been that caring and compassionate leader to me and my family who all belonged to the Israel CME Church. During my college years at Purdue University Calumet campus in Hammond, Indiana, he was always there for special events and provided scholarship aid and opportunities to preach and minister in the church. During the illness and passing of all of my family members, he was present at the hospital and throughout the bereavement period. Throughout my mother's extensive illness, he never forgot to visit her and kept me informed of her condition as I resided in another city presiding as Bishop.

Rev. Dr. Cargle served as a role model not only in a pastoral position but in his role as Presiding Elder of Gary and the Chicago District. He was instrumental in Encouraging, Equipping, Empowering men and women for successful ministry in the CME Church. He certainly was outstanding as a pastor and presiding elder relating to the community and make sure they were aware of the CME Church and its many great achievements. There were no major events and organizations such as the Ministerial Alliance of Gary, the Urban League, NAACP, political gatherings and the school system where he was not involved. He is truly a community activist of the highest magnitude with the gifts and graces to share and communicate effectively across the denominational and racial

Four Pillars of Society

lines. He could always represent the best interest of the African American community and bring much needed resources for the total City of Gary.

When he became the presiding elder of the Chicago District appointed by Bishop D.I. Isom, Jr., he began an extensive training from 9am-2pm on Saturday for all pastors and especially ministers who had newly received their call to preach or who had been assigned pastors for the first time. He required that they know and respect the [3] main books of Methodist; Bible, Hymnal, Discipline along with our CME History so that we could be properly balanced in our preaching, teaching, counseling, and stewardship of our church to make sure that we were fulfilling financial obligations for all three levels: local, district, and annual conferences. He left no stone unturned for the laity of the church as he trained and properly informed them of their role in their local church – learning to work with their pastor; developing a yearly calendar and budget for the church.

When we began One Church One School (OCOS) Community Partnership Outreach in Chicago in 1994, he was our Presiding Elder at the Carter Temple CME Church. He joined laying a solid foundation as he worked with me and Dr. Phedonia Johnson to create a viable and effective ministry. Later when the OCOS ministry began to go regionally and nationally in our great Zion, he, along with the help of Bishop D.I. Isom, made sure it was endorsed by the General Conference of the CME Church. He now serves as the National Vice President of OCOS and has been instrumental in spreading across racial and denominational lines so that all the faith community share our focus...*Value Life and Value Learning.* Truly this book addresses the [4] Pillars of Society; Family, School, Church, Community, and should be required reading for all Christians who want to make a positive and sustained contribution for our church and world.

Bishop Henry M. Williamson, Sr.
Presiding Prelate of the First Episcopal District
Chairman of the College of Bishops (2018-2019)

PILLAR I: The Family

Pictured above is my grandfather, Elder J. M. Cargle and other family members, including my siblings and myself.

PILLAR I: The Family

> **To Husband and Wife**
> Preserve sacredly the privacies of your own house, your married state and your heart.
> Let no one ever presume to come between you or share the joys or sorrows that belong to you two alone.
> With mutual help, build your quiet world, not allowing your dearest earthly friend to be the confidant of aught that concerns your domestic peace.
> Let moments of alienation, if they occur, be healed at once. Never, never speak of it outside; but to each other confess, and all will come out right.
> Never let the morrow's sun still find you at variance.
> Renew and renew your vow. It will do you good and thereby your minds will grow together contented in that love which is stronger than death and you will be truly one.
> *Author Unknown*

God Created the Family

In the book of the beginning, Genesis, we read how the earth was without form. We read that the earth was dark and that there was no shape. Out of the darkness and the implied pointlessness of the earth, God decided to design a world which would alleviate the hopelessness described within the text. We read how God, in an extremely systematic manner created the heavens, the sun, moon and stars. The Genesis account describes how each day the victory of creation gave rise to some new and wonderful imagination of the Creator. Still, within all the splendor and beauty elevated within the account something was yet lacking.

God looked across His creation and said, "I am lonely. I will make me a man." This notion of loneliness, as accounted in the poetry of James Weldon Johnson "The Creation" is

PILLAR I: The Family

something to consider. Why would God need to keep company with something less compatible to Himself?

> "So God created man in his own image, in the image of God created he him; Male and female created he them." (Genesis 1:27) "And God blessed them, and God said unto them, be fruitful and multiply, and replenish the earth, and subdue it; and have dominion over the fish of the sea and over the fowl of the air, and over every living thing that moves upon the earth." (Genesis 1:28)

God created Adam on the sixth day of creation and man is the grand climax of all that God accomplished in His Creation. In the final act of Creation, the creation of man, we observe that God chose to join the material and immaterial parts for man. Man's body was shaped from the dust of the earth, but he became a living soul only after God breathed the breath of life into his nostrils. Man's first response to God was to live.

Psalm 8:1 states, "Oh Lord our Lord how excellent is thy name in all the earth. When I consider the moon and the stars, what is man that Thou art mindful of him?" What is man indeed? So completely devoted to man is God, He organized and establishes codes by which, if followed, man's life would be full and communion with the Almighty secure. The first dispensation, the Divine Ordering of affairs, innocence (pure and without sin), was governed by the Edenic Covenant. This creative covenant between the Triune God who serves as the first party and the newly created man who serves as the second party, regulated man's dominion and subjugation of the earth and presented a simple test of obedience. The penalty of disobedience was death.

Under this covenant relationship for Adam and Eve, God gave six obligations:
1. To replenish the earth with children.

PILLAR I: The Family

2. To use nature for their physical needs including food and shelter.
3. To have dominion over animal life.
4. To eat fruits and vegetables.
5. To labor for their sustenance.
6. To obey God by abstaining from eating the forbidden fruit.

These six basic instructions were given to the first parents, Adam and Eve by God. God gave to the first parents; Adam and Eve this set of foundational goals and therefore they become transferable to all families.

God, established, if you will, a code of conduct by which all families of the earth should operate. God delegated husbands to lead their families and that wives would work with their husbands in cooperation to obtain goals developed within the six basic instructions. Parents teach their children daily by example to be responsible in reaching the goals established within the covenant. These goals will help each family build a strong work ethic and to respect the relationships they develop with others who are made in the image of God.

These images of God are responsible for populating the world. We understand God is creative, orderly, custodial and full of grace. In God's creation, He provided for all of the basic needs for mankind. God created plants in nature for physical food and shelter. God has given man responsibility to have dominion over animal life. He provided Adam, via direct instruction in the Garden, knowledge on how to train the animals and how to use them for the preservation of family life. God knew that family members needed food to eat and he planted fruit trees and made available a variety of vegetables for them to eat.

God knew that mankind needed work to do and he created a vast world where there would be much work to be done. God put man in charge. He made man in His image to be in charge of the whole world. The authority of God abided within the man who had been created. In order for the world to become livable, God taught man how to organize the work force, the family, in order to accomplish God's objectives. God patterned for man his expectations through the productivity of creation. God's expectation of order is proclaimed there. God himself models what fruitfulness looks like within the complexity and variety of nature. God's exemplification of multiplying spiritual relationships is evidenced within His self-counsel proclamation, "Let us make Man." The unity of God achieved in creation.

The Authority of Man
Man is expected to continue this unity through the development of families, schools, churches, and community. I asked myself, *why did God wait until He had finished with all his creations before creating Adam? And why did God create Eve after Adam had completed the task of naming each animal? Did God anticipate some division between the man and woman during the task?* Think about how difficult it was for you to name your children. How difficult was it for you and your spouse to settle on a name?

God delegated Adam to assume the awesome responsibility of having dominion and showing leadership over all creation. Perhaps after the woman is presented there would be a fundamental proof of his authority as he communicated to her how God had allowed him to name all that was created and whatever name he gave, God accepted. Think about the scene. Think about the authority received and accepted when you boast of some accomplishment you've made to your mate or someone you are seeking to impress!

PILLAR I: The Family

God knew that it was now time for Adam to have a help mate, a wife.

> "And the Lord God caused deep sleep to fall upon Adam, and he slept: and he took one of his ribs, and closed up the flesh instead thereof; And the rib, which the Lord God had taken from man, made him a woman, and brought her unto the man. And Adam said; This is now bone of my bones, and flesh of my flesh, she shall be called Woman, because she was taken out of Man. Therefore shall a man leave his father and his mother, and shall cleave unto his wife and they shall be one flesh. And they were both naked, the man and his wife, and were not ashamed." (Genesis 2:21-25)

The Bible makes it clear that God's plan for marriage is one man for one woman for one lifetime. God's gift to man, a wife to help care for all that God has provided.

Marriage is so important in the mind of God that it was the first of three divine institutions and was patterned to illustrate Christ's love for the church. Adam becomes the father of all creation, the father of mankind, the first man to be married, the husband of Eve, and father of many generations. God's pattern for martial happiness is evident when a man loves and leads his family, with children who obey and revere their parents.

What the Bible says about Marriage:

- Marriage is God's Idea (Genesis 2:18-24)
- Commitment is essential to a successful marriage (Genesis 24:58-60)
- Romance is important (Song of Songs 4:9-10)
- Marriage holds time of great joy (Jeremiah 33:10-11)
- Marriage creates the best environment for raising children (Malachi 2:14-15)
- Unfaithfulness breaks the bond of trust, the foundation of all relationships (Matthew 5:22)

PILLAR I: The Family

- Marriage is permanent (Matthew 19:6)
- Ideally, only death should dissolve marriage (Romans 7:2-3)
- Marriage is based on the principled practice of love, not on feelings (Ephesians 5:21-33)
- Marriage is a living symbol of Christ and the Church (Ephesians 5:23, 32)
- Marriage is good and honorable (Hebrews 13:4)
  Scriptural quotes from the Application Bible

Family Life

In the community where we lived most of the people were farmers. My dad never was too much of a farmer. His friends would tell him "Y.J. with all of the twelve (12) children you have, you should be farming more land." Dad's major concern was building a foundation for his family, and he just didn't see that in farming.

Dad had other interest for his children. He envisioned some of us owning a grocery store or owning a Gulf service station, becoming carpenters, or working as community activists. Dad saw that farming was alright for those who could not do any better. Dad and mother had a greater calling for their children. 1) To stay grounded in the body of Christ, 2) stay in school, 3) get a good education, 4) respect people of all races, and 5) to stay focused on what you want to become in life.

Webster's New World Dictionary defines the family as all of the people living in the same household, consisting of parents, and children that they rear, relatives and a group of people related by ancestry of marriage; relatives.

The Family conceivably, is the first school for children. It is within the nucleus of many families that the first teachings of God are conveyed. These teachings consist of concepts for the development of responsibility, love, respect, sharing, discipline, and obedience. These foundational concepts are

PILLAR I: The Family

integral parts of building relationships in family, school, church, and community. These institutions are responsible for teaching the difference between right and wrong. It is important that each institution understand its responsibility while preparing individuals to become well rounded persons who are able to contribute to the community in which they reside.

> "Train Up a child in the way he should go: and when he is old he will not depart from it." (Proverbs 22:6)

Proverbs 22:6 communicates to us that the first training ground is the family. Children are able to develop a sense of purpose, worth and expectation based upon the leadership of their parents. Parents impart a sense of identity to their children as they train and develop their dependency on God.

The King James Study Bible Old English verbiage of, "Train up a child", refers to the total process of molding a child's life. The word train comes from the Vulgar Latin word root 'traginare' or 'tragere,' meaning to put in the mouth, and implies for the idea of conditioning the palate. Parental training should help children develop a taste for the things of God. The home is a preparatory school for life, a cultural center of understanding. Proverbs subscribes to the ancient law which demands honor for one's father and mother.

Biblical teaching of effective parental training emphasizes a balance on instruction and discipline. The parents are the first teachers, not the school or the church. It is the responsibility of the parents to teach the basic skills of life: how to talk, how to pray, how to read, how to eat balanced meals, how to form relationships, to have respect for others, to be honest, and to understand the notion of consequence. Thus, they will be able to discern right and wrong decisions, to love their family, and to take care of their personal belongings. Parents have done well if they are able to teach their children how to provide for their spiritual, physical, emotional, social, and financial needs.

Paul makes it clear in the book of Ephesians:

> "Children, obey your parents in the Lord: for this is right. Honour thy father and mother; (which is the first commandment with promise) That it may be well with thee, and thou mayest live long on the earth. And, ye fathers, provoke not your children to wrath: but bring them up in the nurture and admonition of the Lord." (Ephesians 6:1-4 *KJSB*)

The parents have the responsibility of teaching their children in an environment where character, education, respect, responsibility, and relationships are taught daily in the home. These are the basic foundations that are necessary for all children to receive in early childhood.

Parents need to understand they have the responsibility to instruct their children on understanding rules and laws that are to be enforced with punishment applied when these laws are broken. It is imperative that children understand authority. It is imperative that they understand why it is they must submit to authority within the concept of society. Love is the foundation by which all teaching must be rooted. Without love, children may see teaching as unreasonable and brutal.

Seemingly, the idea of submitting to authority is an altogether forgotten notion within the context of modern society. Modern day conflicts between children, parents and authority figures reflect a greater need for parents to train and equip children to respect and engage persons in authority.

PILLAR I: The Family

Meal and Teaching Time

Now more than ever, parents must assume the responsibility for preparing their children for the years ahead. It is from this training children receive the tools they need in order for them to develop successfully from early childhood, to adolescence, to adulthood. Training up children is a comprehensive responsibility that includes nurturing with clear directions, plans, goals, and objectives which enable children to achieve the best out of life.

I have watched many parents who wanted to make all of the choices and decisions for their children believing they were sparing pain and canceling sorrow for them. This style of parenting will hurt the child in the long run. When parents teach their children how to make decisions, they don't have to watch every step they take. Many times children form the opinion that 'they are grown.' They feel they don't need their parents always checking on them. They feel they can make their own decisions, and they are right in some cases. The children whose parents have taught them about life, who have nurtured maturity and created opportunities for

PILLAR I: The Family

wisdom develop children who are able to problem solve and are usually able to make wise choices.
In his book, **Better Dads, Stronger Sons**, Rick Johnson concludes, "Fathers have an innate ability to influence their children and the community around them. " He calls it "father power." This power is from God and it allows fathers to affect people's lives positively or negatively, for good or evil, for hundreds of years." (Johnson, R. 2006, p. 31)

Parents cannot completely turn their children loose, because of the love they have for them. Parents must trust they have molded their children's lives from their conception towards independence. Parents must pray that their children will be successful in completing their spiritual, educational, social, vocational, and marital goals.

Parents have the responsibility of setting guidelines and boundaries to ensure their children's future will be productive. Through appropriate modeling, the children have a point of reference for the offspring they will nurture. The Bible gives this responsibility to parents, not police officers, not teachers, nor pastors, or social workers; but to parents! Although those other authority figures play a major role, it should be in supporting the foundations that parents have laid. It is their professional duty to make sure they too are committed to the development of the children's professional goals in the context of parental secondary resources.

In his recently published book, **The Vanishing American Adult**, Senator Ben Sasse calls families back to these family practices as well. Senator Sasse says parents must develop distractions from day to day peer pressure by engaging with their children during meal time gatherings. Parents should be involved with their children in order to communicate household expectations for unity and achievement. I believe in order for us to regain the family, we must go back to the

practice of family. Families are strong when we work to build them through interaction. (Sasse, B. 2017)
As a result of following my parent's teaching, their children's goals were met. All of their children were able to find good jobs, and stayed involved in the church. It was the desire of our parents that all of the children would work to receive certification, to graduate from high school, GED, attend college and perhaps work towards advanced degrees: LPN, BS, MA, MS and PhD's.

We saw our mother and father involved in the church. Mother was a member of the Stewardess Board and Missionary Society. Dad was a member of the choir, a Trustee of the Church, and also served on the Steward Board. Dad also served as a Trustee for our school and was a community activist. Our parents planted the seed within us that we could achieve beyond their accomplishments. We had conversations regarding educational practices which helped lead us to become licensed practicing nurses, teachers, ministers, accountants, and technical operators. Some of my siblings followed our Dad by becoming entrepreneurs; by developing real-estate agencies, owning laundromats and dry cleaners, and operating BBQ restaurants.

These teachings and conversations persisted into to the next generation. All of the children's children graduated from high school or obtained certification for technical jobs, and many of them went on to become college graduates. Still others have earned advanced degrees in various fields, such as Law, Medicine, Business, and the Fine Arts.

Guided Practice
Our parents taught us respect for each other, in the home by example. They taught us that there would be order and respect in their house. We were taught that somebody was in charge at all times. When our mother and father had to leave

PILLAR I: The Family

the house for any reason the oldest child was in charge. We knew that, and we understood that was the rule of our house, because Mother and Dad had made those rules and we knew that Dad was always ready to enforce those rules. We knew the consequences when a rule was broken and the report was given to Mother and Dad when they returned home. We knew that Dad would ask us, "Is it true that you didn't' do what was asked of you by the one in charge?"

Dad always allowed us to explain what happened. When we had finished our explanation, if it didn't sound right, Dad would reach for the razor strap hanging on the kitchen door and we knew what was next. We often talked about the whippings Dad gave us. Back then, if the child abuse laws had been in effect, then most fathers would have been jailed.

My mother and father had twelve children, and I was the youngest. "He that spares his rod hates his son: but he that loves him chastens him in season." (Proverbs 13:24 *NKJSB)* We knew that our parents loved us, because they taught us how to love, and to respect others at all times. Those instructions were instilled in us and wherever we went those rules followed us. Whether we were on the playground or in the fields, or in town, or at church or in school, we were reminded that we were representatives of the Cargle family, and not to tarnish the Cargle name.

> "A good name is more desirable than great riches; to be esteemed is better than silver or gold." (Proverbs 22:1 *NIV*)

In our home we were taught there was a timely relationship for everything. We ate breakfast, lunch and supper together, and we blessed the food with family prayer. Each person had to repeat a Bible verse. You ate whatever food that was prepared. In our house there was no concept of not liking any food served; or not liking what was on the table. To put it

PILLAR I: The Family

plainly, there was no eating out. You ate what was cooked and expressed how you enjoyed the meal. I remember one morning we were eating oatmeal for breakfast, and the oatmeal was bitter, so I asked Dad why was the oatmeal so bitter, and Dad said, "It was simple boy, the cows were in the fields and they ate bitter weeds and wild onions, whatever cows eat the taste will come through the milk and butter."

I remember dad saying that in the thirties, and I have thought about it many times. My dad was not a rocket scientist, if he knew back in the thirties, why has it taken scientists so long to discover that if a woman or man smokes cigarettes, or marijuana, uses drugs, and drinks hard whisky, it is possible that the effects of negative indulgences might come through the sperm or woman's blood stream and affect the baby. A woman's womb is sacred; it is the holy place where seeds grow and therefore we must minimize at risk behavior through education.

You didn't come to mother and dad's table with dirty hands and faces, half dressed with pants down to your knees, shirts unbuttoned, mad, looking foolish and behaving disrespectfully to the people at the table. We were taught that meal time was a sacred time for order in the house and where major decisions and discussions took place regarding the family chores, school progress and current events. Our discussions would continue at evening time while having *family show time*. That was when each family member had to recite a scripture, a poem, sang a song, you had to make up something to say or act out. This may sound a bit old fashioned to some, but we bonded with each other in a very real and personal way.

Each family member would encourage each other with applause when the act was completed. Refreshments were always available. We shared in the eating of popcorn, roasted peanuts, drinking Kool-Aid, and just having plain old family fun at show time. Often, after all of the popcorn and peanuts were eaten, some of the family members would hide some of their popcorn and peanuts and then tease the others by showing what they had. Even after the teasing was over, we would always share treats we had hidden with one another.

Value of a Father and a Mother

My father and mother taught us about life, mental hygiene, getting a good education, staying out of trouble, and making something out of ourselves. They taught us to never be satisfied with fairly good, pretty good, or good enough; accepting nothing other than our best. This was the law in our home.

Mother taught us boys and girls how to keep house and how to cook. Mother was an excellent cook. She could take nothing and make something out of it. Mother knew how to take the left overs and make a good meal. She would take black eyed peas that were left over from supper, and make Black Eyes Peas Croquettes for breakfast. She mashed the black eye peas, added salt, green pepper, eggs, onion, celery, and mixed all ingredients together, dust flower or corn meal over the croquettes and put them in a skillet and cook them until they were brown on both sides.

Mother was gifted in making so many dishes that were good eating for a large family including her grandchildren and nieces. Mother taught us how to wash, iron and fold clothes. Mother stated that it was important for the boys to learn how to cook and keep house because the wife may become ill one day.
Parents meant what they taught, you knew they loved you and they wanted you to become somebody. So the saying was "spare the rod you spoiled the child." The father was the man in charge. When he spoke the house came to order. Because

PILLAR I: The Family

we knew he was the man of the house and he spoke with authority and we knew that he would use his authority. That is one of the major issues in many homes today.

No Longer Being Complacent and Passive

We see there are too many homes where the male voice is absent. There is no father that speaks with authority. Too many Black family homes are suffering and divided because there is a lack of a father figure. Boys need a father or a male image to talk to them, and teach them about developing from boyhood to manhood. Fathers are needed to relate to them about the facts of life.

Mychal Denzel Smith writes in his book *Invisible Man, Got the Whole World Watching: A Young Black Man's Education,* "So much of the understanding of what liberation for black people looked like was predicated on the notion of the patriarchal model of family -- that when black men, unencumbered by racism, were allowed to return to their rightful place as head of a household with their wives and children, we would, as a race truly be free."
(Smith, M. 2016, p. 162)

Identity is vital within the concept of family. Everyone within the home should know who they are and why they are essential to the household. Men, with women, are able to establish balance and identity for their children. But these concepts must be nurtured early. Parents who fail to help children develop and establish an identity within the home will have children who later fail to cope within social world constructs.

Let the children know that as a parent you are willing to teach them how to deal with peer pressure, temptation, dating, loneliness and mood swings. Too often mothers and fathers form the opinion that all their children want is more things

PILLAR I: The Family

and clothes. Once you give them their weekly allowance that's it. Not so. Could it be and maybe what they need is your time, love, touch, hugs and embraces? Your care and touch allow them to know that you love them; that you are their friend and parent. You are available to listen to them at any time. How much quality time are you spending with your children? Children seek genuine affection from mothers and yes, from fathers too. It may seem that the world seeks to remove fathers from the home, but we can affirm the power of a father's love and guidance through our own examples.

Social needs and how to respect others

Puberty is a time consisting of rapid physical growth and changes which can seem to be both exciting and confusing. It's a time of questioning and learning, but most of all, growing. The years when you first become physically able to create a baby have been reported as usually 9 – 14 years of age. Mentally; You'll think new thoughts and consider new ideas. Emotionally, you may feel happier and sadder than ever before, and you may care about others in new ways, too. Socially, you'll act differently around other people like a grown-up, and less like a "little kid." Parents should teach their children about the facts of life and help them to work through their emotional, spiritual, and social needs.

Girls and women are not to be treated like boys or men, despite what they may see on rap videos. Boys need to be trained how to treat a girl when going out on a date. They need to understand that you come in the home to pick up the young lady instead of blowing your car horn for her to come out and simply opening the car door for her to jump in. Boys and young men need to know that they should escort, protect, and look after her needs when she is out with you. As important as it is to train up young ladies in how to deal with young men, it is essential and imperative that young men are

PILLAR I: The Family

trained how to treat young ladies, especially in the Black community.

If your children want to spend more time in the streets with their friends, then what quality time are they spending with you? You'd better check that out. Street kids may be winning your children over and robbing them of all their hopes and dreams. If you want to protect your investment and guard the dreams of your child, then you have to pour into their lives. As a concerned father and mother you need to know why your child has fallen in love with the kids on the streets, next door, across town.

You must investigate why they don't want to come home, and when they do come home they lock their door, turn on the TV, begin texting those they just left about what they will do next when they meet again. Somebody has too much influence over your children's schedule. If this is a pattern that is taking place 24 hours a day and 7 days a week in your home, you better call an emergency meeting to regain control of your child or children, before the street elements have control of them.

Gary Chapman, Ph.D. and Ross Campbell, M.D. have identified five love languages for us: *physical touch; words of affirmation; quality time; gifts; and acts of service.* In order to develop successfully within a family, each component must be actualized. Children who experience each are able to provide the same for their offspring and are bonded for life to that which accentuates well roundedness.

There is a great deal to be gained by godliness. Our spiritual needs enable us to press on to higher goals, because we have that glue that binds us to the Body of Christ. Our physical health is susceptible to disease and injury, but faith can sustain us through these tragedies. As parents we must learn

PILLAR I: The Family

to develop the gifts that God has given to us by applying and teaching them to our children and the community where we live.

The *Matthew Henry Commentary* says, "The promises made to godly people relate to the life that now is, but especially the promises of God for godly people are relatable to the life that is to come." (1 Timothy 4:7- 8) Parents train their children to expect the rewards of God through right relationship as found in the Edenic principals established for families by God.

Emotional Needs

Moses and Aaron were the leaders who were charged to lead a community of people into a new land, a new community where opportunities would be better for all. Because of their lack of trust and faith in God they allowed fear and frustration to break out on their journey to a new community. When confusion and despair broke out in the camp, their greatest fears were losing their perspective and feeling ill prepared to complete their journey because the people were caught up in their emotions, fears, and had forgotten about God's blessings.

People get caught up in false reports, not getting the correct information, making decisions based upon what they heard coming from unreliable sources, and in many cases from individuals who are not creditable in the community. These individuals have a way of persuading people, when they know in their hearts they are not telling the truth. Fearful people will accept a lie before they accept the truth. Fearful people are often those who cannot trust anyone, not even God. They are unable to make decisions because they are fearful about everything, and they will find it impossible to make important decisions. It is imperative for parents to help their children understand as they grow and develop into various stages of life, it is normal for them to have some emotional fears about

PILLAR I: The Family

some of the decisions they will make in life. The lesson of overcoming fear is a continuous lesson.
President Franklin D. Roosevelt once said, "...the only thing we have to fear is...fear itself." It is imperative for parents to help their children overcome fear and their emotions by spending quality time, explaining and walking them through the various stages children go through. They may have low self-esteem, insecurities of not knowing who they are, or where they are going; as in Exodus 4:10, afraid of going forward to Canaan when it is easier to look again to Egypt.

Parents may reassure their children they love them, not in just words but sharing their love at all times, at home, during bed time reading together and sharing stories that make sense to the child. Always find out how your child is doing in school, with homework, school activities that your child is involved in, and the role you as a father and mother may play in helping your child to achieve a quality education and a well-adjusted life with other children who are enrolled in school and those who are in their community.

Parents have been there. Parents owe it to their children to help them understand that emotional insecurities are a part of life. They need not fear the way they look, the way they sound when they talk, their body size, or their need to feel and to touch to explore their bodies. Those needs come as children develop growing pains; making adjustments into adulthood.

As parents and leaders who are concerned about the welfare of our children and family, we have a role that we must employ at all times. We as adults need to display our spiritual and physical selves before our children and the community at all times. Our spiritual needs are those things that make us happy and fit to enjoy the best of life. Physical needs are important; however, in my opinion if the body has all its godliness, faith, love, confession, repentance and goodwill toward all people, the harmony of both the physical and spiritual will be made whole.

We must learn daily to train our thoughts, our deeds by following the teaching of our Lord and Savior Jesus Christ. The teaching of Jesus instructs us to meditate daily on his words and be inspired by using His words as a guide each day to help us on our journey. Faith helps us to maintain a closer walk with God, and this comes with our involvement in churches, and schools where we teach and touch the lives of others who are on the faith journey.

Society's Role in Supporting Families

When both entities are working together, family and community play a major role in reaching the social needs of each family member. When parents have a positive attitude toward the children's need within the community, communities are empowered to grow to their fullest potential. There are many factors beyond the parent-child relationship that affect the ability to care for children.

Parents need basic resources such as food, clothing, housing, transportation, and access to essential services that address family specific needs (such as child care and health care) to ensure the health and wellbeing of their children.

Some families may also need support connecting to social services such as alcohol and drug treatment centers, domestic violence counseling, or public health benefits. Providing or connecting families to the concrete supports that families need is critical. These combined efforts help families cope with stress and prevent situations where maltreatment could occur.

PILLAR I: The Family

These *protective factors* are critical for all parents and caregivers, regardless of the child's age, sex, ethnicity or racial heritage, economic status, special needs, or whether he or she is raised by a single, married or divorced parent or other caregivers. All of these factors work together to reinforce each other. For example, parents are more likely to be resilient in times of stress when they have social connections and a strong attachment to their child. Protective factors can provide a helpful conceptual framework for providers working with children and their families.

Understanding the role that social factors play, as well as interventions that work to address them may improve our ability to plan and implement effective prevention polices. Parent partnerships work when many parents are consistently involved as decision makers in program planning, implementing, and assessment. Suggestions for implementing parent partnerships:

- *Partner with parent organizations*
- *Create and maintain prominent leadership roles for parents*
- *Learn about what motivates parents to engage in program leadership*
- *Provide leadership training and support for parents.*
- *Creates opportunities for parents to engage directly around the protective factors.*
- *Designate specific resources for parent engagement, participation, and leadership.*

We understand that these are critical times for parents and family members as they work hard to maintain their home, mortgage payment, supporting their church tithes/offerings, school activities for their children, food expenses, car notes, utilities, and clothing cost. All of these are bare necessities in keeping a standard of living for the average family.

PILLAR I: The Family

Many families are hurting today and this is the reason we need to be aware of the social agencies that are available to give assistance. Sometimes, hard times bring families and communities together to share what they have. Years ago family members knew the people who lived down the road, or across the road, or down the street, or over the hill, or in the next village. Families knew family members by names, and they knew the children of that family and would correct them when they did something wrong, and reported it to their parents. Children were taught how to speak, and how to say "Good morning", "Good afternoon, how are you feeling to day Mr. Target or Mrs. Target?" "It's a beautiful day and it looks like it's going to rain tomorrow." Children knew how to converse with others they interacted with.

We were taught to say "Yes Sir" and "Yes Ma'am" to all older people we met as a sign of respect. We were taught to step back and hold the door when senior citizens walked toward you, because they had the right away. It was a village where people were concerned about family members. They shared what they had. News got around from family to family, if any family needed anything; their needs were met with compassion and with understanding. There was no bullying at schools or teasing the children who were in need. The source of comfort back in the day for families in need was the community. The community was a social service agency. We helped each other because we belonged to one another.

Parents Advocate for Their Children
School was open Monday through Friday, for only a few months out of the year because of planting and harvest seasons. This fact made it very hard to find teachers who were willing to come to a rural school district. As it turned out, there were only a few teachers who met the requirements. I am reminded that these schools were housed in the Black churches. The pastor and trustees of the churches

PILLAR I: The Family

provided the building, utilities and the county Board of education provided the salary for the teachers.

I can remember my father preparing the church building for Sunday worship and for Public School at Ebenezer C.M.E. Church in Hillsboro, Alabama. I can remember my dad calling a group of fathers together and organizing them to meet with the superintendent to provide a public school building as they had done for whites. My dad and the committee also requested they provide bus transportation for the children who had to walk more than two miles to school. The committee advised the superintendent there was a building in the community that was built for white missionaries and it was never used. And also, there was a small building that was built and it was never used. The school board and the superintendent accepted their recommendations.

> "The effectual fervent prayer of a righteous man availeth much."
> James 5:16

The Black families throughout Hillsboro, Alabama rejoiced in the Lord knowing that a milestone had been accomplished as their children were now able to secure a better education, in a building that was equipped to handle student enrollment from grades first to twelve, with better teachers, library books, bus transportation, a lunchroom, and sports programs which were included in the school curriculum. This was in the year 1937. The name of the school was chosen: Tennessee Valley High School.

The community was very happy and delighted and expressed their appreciation to my father who was the chairman of the committee and others. My mother and father were delighted because six of their children were enrolled in the school. Those six were Josie, Frank, Sidney, Alma, Elmer and me, (Carrell). I graduated in the class of 1949 and applied for the work study program to attend Alabama State College for Negroes, now Alabama State University.

In June of 1949 I was accepted and worked in President Trenholm's office until I graduated in1953. As a full time student working during the summer months I was paid $.30 per hour full time, and $.15 per hour during class time. The work study program dollars were credited toward tuition and board, no check was issued to me. My sister Alma worked in the president's1office and graduated from Alabama State College for Negroes, which open the opportunity for me to work there. My sister Alma was very supportive to me, by sending me a check each month for $10.00, and that was the salvation in those college days. Remember I told you earlier, parents share in the dreams of their children.

Taking advantage of your networks

Because my father died in 1946 and he was a member of Prince Hall AFM Mason, I was awarded a four years scholarship toward my tuition. While in college I became very active on campus because of my involvement in the work study program which gave me a jump start to meet all of the administrators, teachers, staff members and the students who were attending summer school and the incoming freshman class. This put me into a leadership role on campus.

I became involved in the Student Council, President of the Marshall Club, member of the Alpha Phi Alpha fraternity, dean of pledges and the religious Council. I graduated in 1953, with a Bachelor of Science Degree in Social Studies. My experience in working out of the President's office gave me the opportunity to observe the President, his administrative staff, and see how decisions were made and implemented in the working process. This was an educational learning process that helped to mold me into the leader that I have become.

PILLAR I: The Family

Black men in the Rural South

It was the Black men in the rural south that brought about change. These men worked from sun up to sun down on land they were renting or trying to purchase. These strong Black men were determined to make a way for their families. The fathers used their leadership to teach their children how to plant seeds, to produce vegetables for harvesting, and how to raise chickens and hogs to be used for feeding the family. Black men in the rural south modeled for us how to cultivate seeds for your own success. They never wanted us to become trapped inside of systems of bondage.

Too many fathers and young men are trapped in jails and prisons presently. Trapped people develop links with others who are trapped. These links create a dysfunction within their community. Neighborhoods become war zones. Concerned citizens exit from these death zones to neighborhoods where there is hope.

When I look at the Black community I have seen outstanding names that have been tarnished because of disgruntled negative people. Church names tarnished because of disgruntled pastors and church members. Schools tarnished because of disgruntled, teachers, staff, parents and students. Public buildings, parks, and street signs, tarnished because of disgruntled workers, and disgruntled street gangs that are fighting over territorial rights. Family names tarnished because of a bad divorce and in- law fighting, names of businesses tarnished because of disgruntled employees.

While other fathers and mothers sought the opportunity of teaching their children the value of getting a good education in school, vocational training or college, Dad first taught us our name was important, and not to tarnish the name "Cargle." Tarnished means to deface, to cover up, to make it look bad, to lose its identity, to stain, blemish.

PILLAR I: The Family

It's time for us to take a critical look in our community, where we live, our houses of worship, our schools and businesses: Are they reaching the needs of the people who reside in those communities? Have we allowed the tarnishing concept to become one of the driving forces that are destroying families, and the very community that our parents sacrificed to build on their knees, working from sun up to sun down on farm land and plantations?

Fathers and mothers built their homes, raised their children, laid the foundation for their children not to be satisfied just getting by on the farm land. Stay in school, study hard, and get a good education and make something out of yourselves. "Be somebody we can be proud of. " A goal you must achieve! Churches, schools, businesses were built by sacrificing pennies, nickels and dimes. Today, most families make more money in one month than parents made in a year. How did they do it? They did it on relationships and commitment, prayer, faith, hope, God will make a way somehow.

Parents and institutions of higher learning help shape the world's future by the way they shape their children's values. The first step toward helping children live rightly is for parents to live rightly before their children. Parent's actions are often copied by those closed to them. What kind of example are you setting for your children? The family needs everyone to function effectively.

What a person will become, and how successful, they will become is determined by each person's relationship with his or her family, church school, community, and government are the foundations that keep relationships glued together, and bring about positive changes. Successful relationship is a together that moves people in helping them to reach their goals, overcoming misguided information, negative thoughts,

PILLAR I: The Family

low self-esteem and lack of knowledge to understand what is right or wrong in the sight of God.

What Happened to Big Mommy and Uncle Joe?

Big Mommy and Uncle Joe were the foundations of many Black families. Big Mommy and Uncle Joe were the kind of people who lived in every neighborhood years ago. I am using the names of Big Mommy and Uncle Joe for what they stood for and the way they communicated to members of the family and people in general. It was not because of their physical sizes, big or small, married or single, it was what they stood for.

They had a gift from God, and when they spoke the house came to order. They earned that respect because they were always seen as caring for and providing for the needs of the people. They were respected by family members and neighbors. In the community they had a divine way of telling what the people needed to hear. They knew when to speak and where to speak under a divine order from God. Big Mommy is not a woman who thrived on negative conversation or one who was always dipping into family matters or business. Big Mommy was the bearer of wisdom.

Her mind stayed on Jesus

Big Mommy showed up when God spoke to her. God would tell her in a dream or vision to go next door, or call a person or family members and tell them what they needed to hear. Whenever she would walk through the neighborhood, all of the children and neighbors respected her, and passed the word that Big Mommy was coming by. She knew how to enter into a family relationship. She knew how to call people together and let them know what the will of God, was telling her to speak "thus says the Lord."

PILLAR I: The Family

Big Mommy would show up whenever there was a divine calling from the Lord to go and console a family who had lost a love one, and she comforted them. She knew how to bring peace and resolve issues when there were misunderstandings. She spoke with a soft voice, with authority penetrating from her lips and moved on the hearts and mind of family members to do what their father, or mother had requested. She knew their parents and each of them by name. She was powerful in her conversations to the family, telling them what they had to do in order to have peace and good will; *you must get that evil spirit and hatred out of your hearts, and out of this house.* All you knew was that your mother and father were Christians, they were known all over this town and state, family members and friends would be coming from everywhere because they have touched so many lives in all walks of life. And you are going to carry out their wishes just as they have left instructions for you to do?

Too many family members today are living in broken relationships, because no one in the family is willing to stand up and tell it like it should be told. However, there are individuals in most families who have the know-how and gift to fill in the gap and call the family together. Sometimes it may be the oldest person who is living, or it may be a middle age or younger person that most of the family members respect.

Family members have broken up because no one is showing any concerns of what needs to be done. Take a look at your family, what do you see? Are all the children doing well in school? Do they have good jobs? Are they prepared for the job market? Are they respectful toward their mother, father, brother or sister, aunt or uncle? How do you view the success of your family members: will they all graduate from high school, trade school and/or college? Will they have a family that will be able to break through the negative curses;

PILLAR I: The Family

overcoming generation fall-out that have touched so many Black families and have caused children to drop out of school, girls having babies, no father to be found to support their babies?

We have too many Black men in jail, absentee mothers and fathers from the family structure triggering major blows to the Black family.

> "Except the Lord build the house, they labour in vain that build it: except the Lord keep the city, the watchman waketh but in vain." Psalm 127:1

> "It is vain for you to rise up early, to sit up late, to eat the bread of sorrow: for so he giveth his beloved sleep." Psalm 127:2

Psalm 127 is written to help the family understand there are four basic principles in building a home for his family. If they don't get these four principles, all efforts are in vain unless they have God's blessing: Building a house, guarding a city, working long hours, having children. It is possible to accomplish all of these things without God's blessings, but it is not possible to accomplish them purposefully and with eternal value without God's blessing.

The Psalm includes, incidentally, two practical reasons for having children: they bring you joy and they protect you. Solomon's ability to understand his father's teaching gave him the foundation that he needed to build his home and family. It's imperative for us to understand if we are going to build a house we must include God in the plan. It is God who gives us the guidance of all details that are to go into the house. We must count the cost.

PILLAR I: The Family

How many rooms

> "Except the Lord build the house, they labour in vain that build it: except the Lord keep the city, the watchman waketh but in vain." (Psalm 127:1)

The sizes for each room are listed on the floor plan of a home. It shows how many bathrooms, bedrooms, closets, guest room, living room, dining room, prayer room, kitchen, laundry room, family room, and library. What type of furniture and appliances are to be selected for each room? Solomon is advising us we must ask God where we should build our home. Count the cost, the location and the type of community before you make your final decision and take it to God. God will show you what is best. Always depend upon God's blessing, and not upon your understanding for building a house and raising a family.

Because of your planning you know what you want in it, you know the cost of each item in each room; you know where you want to build it, upon a hill, or in a valley. You may be proud of all of the architectural design, materials and furniture selected for the house.

Psalm 127:1 says, *"Except the Lord build the house, they labour in vain that build it:"* Meaning there is no purpose for you to build without Him. If the design be laid out on pride, or you built it for the wrong motive, your house will not be blessed. Only God can bless your home. When God blesses your home there will be peace, prosperity, happiness, appreciation, togetherness; a loving relationship with dad, mother and children will reap the benefits.

You will discover when God blesses your home your relationship with your spouse will become a tender and loving situation. Your children will be brought up in a loving home where they see mother and dad are building a

PILLAR I: The Family

relationship that is as solid as a rock. The children see respect, and love for each person in the home.

The children will learn the process of building a home upon the foundation of God. Solomon makes it clear that a house that is built without the approval of God is like a house that is built in a city without a security system, or police protection. This house has no guardian that watches over it 24 hours 7 days a week.

I often asked myself why is it there are so many burglaries, and crimes throughout the city, and especially in the Black communities. Is it because in many homes today, family members are so divided because of broken relationships within the family structure, often due to poverty, lack of education, discipline and a father without compassion of love for his children and family. These many families were not built on the approval of God, and not operating under the guiding hands of our Lord and Savior Jesus Christ.

The police officers cannot secure a city without the guiding hands of God, the support of the family, school, church and community, nor can the good man of the house save his house from being broken into. It takes all working together 24 hours 7 days a week. God is telling us what we must do if we are going to save our investments, and the hours of hard work, on the jobs in order to secure enough money to pay for the material things that have been accumulated for robbers to break in and steal. All resources cannot be affected without the favor of God.

> "It is vain for you to rise up early, to sit up late, to eat the bread of sorrow: for so he giveth his beloved sleep." Psalm 127:2

PILLAR I: The Family

Pictured above is my mother in the center, Josie Cargle, surrounded by my siblings and their spouses.

Rest is very important

God has planned it so that you work so many hours in a day and the remaining hours are for taking care of God's work of teaching family values and advancing God's Kingdom in the home and community. Having children is one of the greatest gifts God has given to a married couple.

"Lo, children are a heritage of the Lord: and fruit of the womb is his reward." Psalm 127:3

"As arrows are in the hand of a mighty man; So are children of thy youth." Psalm 127: 4.

"Happy is the man that hath his quiver full of them: they shall not be ashamed, but they shall speak with the enemies in the gate." Psalms 127: 5. (KJSB)

PILLAR I: The Family

> "And they are to us what we make them, comforts or crosses. Children are a heritage, and a reward, and are so to accounted, blessings and burdens; For he that sends mouths will send meat if we trust in him." Psalm 127: 3.

Children are to be instructed by their parents, brought up in the knowledge of God. They are to be loved, disciplined and trained in the word of God. They are to be taught right and wrong.

Respect for their parents, relatives and all people. They are to be taught the value of their personal property and the properties of others. They are to be given responsibilities of what to do and how to carry them out in the home, school, church and community. Parents are to work with them step by step so they understand how to do it right.

Children love to help their parents do their work when they are growing up. They love to go with their parents, shopping, laundry mats, parks, school functions, vacations and church activities. Parents are to see that their children's school home work and home chores are completed every day. Establish a good loving and working relationship with your children, and this will enable them to come to you when they have questions, about things they just don't understand.

The quality time you spend with your children early on will help determine how successful they will be when they grow up. Quality time is teaching, showing, listening to what they have to say and helping them to work through their questions or problems. Quality time is helping them to understand how to prepare a budget and to live within that budget.
Remember, *"Children are a heritage for the Lord, as well as from him." (Psalm 127:3)*

PILLAR I: The Family

Children should be the product of a loving family, trained in a loving environment, where they are exposed to Christian nurturing, Christian education, integrity, social responsibility, and family relationships. Children that come out of a strong family where parents and children have had a healthy family relationship from the beginning of their marriage through the birth of their first child and the continuation of each additional child brings stability and understanding as mother and father whether the adjustment of a growing family, and sharing their time, and love with each member of the family that is rooted in the joy of a loving God.

A family that has built their relationship with God is a family that knows how to extend their relationships with their family and others. God's relationship doesn't develop toward people based upon how you think they should treat you, or by the way they talk, the way they dress, the way they look, or where they live, their education, sorority, or the influence they have in the community.

God's relationship is a genuine profound connection that is rooted in the blood stream, that enable you to understand that it is the gift of God that has glued your relationship with your kinfolk, and you ought to be grateful that you have relatives and friends that are better off than you are, or you may have relatives you may need to reach out and extend them a helping hand. There are people who will glue themselves to you in order to move out of their situation that held them hostage for years. That's what God's people, clubs, associations and educational advancements are for; to move people into a better way of living.

Building a Bonding Relationship
The Bible says "it is more blessed to give than to receive." Your word is your bond. I don't hear, "Your word is your bond" spoken as people and relatives used to speak it years

ago. It stood for something. It was a commitment. It was an agreement. It was a covenant relationship. You could go to sleep on it. There was a handshake with a grip that meant the agreement lasted until death do us part. A bonding relationship was the glue that God used to tie husband and wife together.

When husbands and wives build a bonded relationship between themselves before their children, it will have an eternal affect upon their children lives from generation to generation. It was a bonding relationship when mothers fed their child from their breast and rocked the baby in her arms to put them to sleep. Mothers extended the bonding experience by whispering prayers at bed side, asking God Almighty to protect her baby while the baby laid down to sleep. Mothers prayed to God to keep the soul of the child in his care. The universal prayer was taught to every child. (Now I Lay Me Down To Sleep…) Parents are responsible for building a strong husband and wife relationship before their children. They show it by speaking kind words to each other, offering respect, showing love toward each other, never verbal or physical abuse toward each other.

I have seen in my pastoral work over sixty years, husband and wife speaking negatively toward each other. I have seen men and women who struggle with anger, personality disorders, low self- esteem, and that often turned their home into a war zone. This type of relationship is detrimental to each person and distrustful to the children and family members. This type of relationship destroys the person you are married to and will have a devastating impact upon your children. As husband and wife you made an agreement with God and each other when you stood before the minister. You were standing in the presence of God.

PILLAR I: The Family

Husbands and wives, I require and charge both of you to be mindful now and always that love is selfless and self-giving one to the other, and loyalty as faithful devotion to each other stand as the foundation of a home that will endure and in which happiness will prevail. You are sealing a bond that is the tenderest among all human bonds, and this vow is the most sacred of all vows.

Bishop Marshall Gilmore, Editor of the CME Pocket Ritual, stated, "If you are careful not to violate these vows and if you will endeavor to do the will of God, your heavenly Father, your life together will abound with joy and your home will be a place of peace."

Black Families Want Change

Some of the changes families make for a better way of life include moving out of neighborhoods of decay and changing the school their children are enrolled in. After relocating into a different community they soon discover the same problems are reoccurring. What's the problem? The problem is Black leadership, pastors, church memberships, fathers, mothers, elected officials, political leaders, schools, community organizers, organizations, educators, business owners, police officers, block clubs and neighborhood watch and children. These persons are stakeholders; whatever is taking place in their communities is coming out of the homes of these persons mentioned.

Family members participated in ministries pertaining to their age group, children and youth ministries, choir, ushering, leading worship service, and other roles that were assigned to enhance the spiritual growth of the family and church membership by participating in weekly activities. Their faithfulness to their God and church, enable them to become a close knitted family. They reared children in the structure of the Bible and kept them actively involved in character building programs.

As the family grew and demands upon mothers and fathers life styles increased, meaning both parents working in the job market and the parents became more involved in the social world and less active in the church. This began to create problems for the whole family. Children became less active in the church and more involved in community activities that were less character building. It has been the Biblical teaching role of parents, schools and Black churches that have kept the community together for many years.

Parents should not allow themselves to live in such an environment. Knowing every day it is the same negative relationship talking about each other, calling each other names that we know that is wrong, disrespectful, abusive and demoralizing. Have they forgotten their wedding vows? Have they forgotten the promise they made when they started standing together and having a family? I have a message to them:

You know what you said; all of that sweet talk you said to each other, and now you are abusing each other every time you look at each other. What about those promises you made, it is about time you live up to them. God is watching you and your children and friends see it all. Now it's time it time to live up to it. It's later than you think. How do you feel when you see your offspring have some of the same problems that you are having? Acting like you, looking like you and talking like both of you. Do you feel guilty? I hope so. Do something about it! For God sake, please do not allow that evil spirit on your children.

Our children deserve a better life, to have a productive relationship with them and their children and a positive relationship with their sibling and family members. Who are

PILLAR I: The Family

you? There are too many families that do not know who they are, and their children are searching for identity, and they will join a gang group in order to find love and happiness. People who are lonely need a bonding relationship with something they can touch, feel and see the right people that will help them to find love, happiness and to be appreciated.

I strongly believe that the leadership and the people should come together and push for the following to occur: Stronger family ties and cohesion; training programs for jobs that are becoming common in the 21st Century; crime reduction and prevention through citizens' initiatives and improvements; improvement in community-police relations and the criminal justice system; more services for the victims of crime; encouraging business and industry to invest more in poor communities; and educational and job training programs for former convicts and for those who are currently incarcerated.

National Prayer from the Family of God

What we need to do is call a mass gathering of prayer warriors, pastors, ministers, educators, community leaders, men, women, political leaders, business leaders, people in all walks of life to come together: The Bible says, "If my people, which are called by my name, shall humble themselves, and pray, and seek my face, and turn from their wicked ways; then will I hear from heaven, and will forgive their sin, and will heal their land." 2 Chronicles 7:14. (KJSB)

God appeared to Solomon in the night as he worked hard to save the land and to unite the people together by coming to the House of Prayer. Solomon had finished building the Temple, for the purpose of having a church house for the people to come and worship. Solomon asked God to make provisions for the people when they sinned. God answered with four conditions for forgiveness:
    1) Humble yourself by admitting your sins.

PILLAR I: The Family

2) Pray to God asking for forgiveness.
3) Seek God continually.
4) And, turn from sinful behavior.

These are four ways of establishing commitments by the people with sincere hearts, minds and spirit as they enter into God's House to pray with all worshipers praying together on one accord, and expecting their prayers to be answered.

Change will come when all God's people: parents, teachers, bishops, pastors, ministers, stewards, deacons, missionaries, prayer warriors, elected officials, politicians, lawyers, sinners, drug pushers, prostitutes, business owners, and community organizers *come together* to worship and pray in time of crises in the community. God promised that he will heal the land. It is now time for the people to be called to the House of Prayer because of their sinful actions and broken relationship with God. God promised,

"If my people who are called by my name humble themselves, and pray and seek my face and turn from their wicked ways, then I will hear from heaven and will forgive their sin and heal their land." 2 Chronicles 7:14

With confession, and repentance from sinful actions of people, God promised harvesting will become fruitful and productive and the land will multiply for the people in the land. We must realize that we are broken.

There is power in the community when citizens from all walks of life humble themselves, come together on one accord, praying for peace in the homes, families, schools, and churches, togetherness for jobs, safe communities, then crime, drugs and unemployment will become of past event. There are forces that are gradually destroying the fabric of

PILLAR I: The Family

our basic institutions: The Family, School, Church, and Community.

I strongly believe when pastors, parents, politicians, business owners community leaders and associations such as, One Church One School, Urban League, NAACP form an active relationship, and partnership with the schools and monitor those students who are showing some behavioral problems in their home and community, and direct those students into Family Wellness Relationship sessions, that will help them to resolve many of the hidden issues that are causing them to lose interest, drop out of school and cause broken relationship with their family members and society.

Many of these students only need a loving paternal image to turn their lives in a positive direction and to find out where their interests are. This will enable the students to get on their right track that will lead them to finding their gifts, and obtain successful goals. Then they can better provide for their families and become those critical civic leaders who can give back to their community.

We have come a long way and have made great progress in many professions ranging from education, journalism, finance, entrepreneurship, politics, entertainment and sports. Many Blacks have become millionaires and a few, like Oprah Winfrey, have even become billionaires.

Many of these successful persons have made it through hard knocks, abusive environments, going in and out of school, jail and prison. They wanted to make a name for themselves knowing that some of them came out of broken homes, raised by single parents, living in the hood where crimes were committed daily in their community. They were determined not to allow any other detouring that would stop them from reaching their dreams.

And because of a strong mother, grandmother, uncle or aunt they were able to achieve the impossible dream by getting involved in after school programs in churches, community centers, Boys and Girls Clubs, Girls and Boys scout, sororities and fraternities sponsoring enrichment programs. Teachers formed a partnership with them by mentoring them in their school assignments and special needs. These organizations and others are committed to helping students and children who are having a hard time succeeding. They are offering programs to help boys and girls to find their interest by keeping them motivated to learn and develop their gifts and talents.

What about those in prison?

In the NWI (North West Indiana) Times News Paper article **"Gary native won't let life in prison deter him from pursuing dreams,"** by Marisa Kwiatkowski (Jun 2, 2013), Charles "Duke" Tanner stated, "If you can't really take some of the worst things that ever happened in your life and do something constructive with them, to me, you're dishonoring the experience that you went through. My situation is the worst of the worst, because I'm sitting in prison with a life sentence. But if I can stand to be positive with that, look at the world on the outside."

There are too many Black men and boys who are in prison with talents and educational skills that could be used in a more productive way than to be rotting away doing nothing. Many of these individuals are smart with their hands, minds and spirit of knowing how to get things accomplished for themselves, their family and government. Just think all of these men and boys that are locked up from their children, wives, family and society. What devastating consequences this has on a race and society.

PILLAR I: The Family

These men are trainable, knowledgeable and are in need of someone to understand them and be willing to give them another chance. In too many instances society has contributed to the sickness that has caused the situation to get to this point. If you look closely, you will see that there is room for improvement by providing Biblical resources, counseling and educational expertise in the home, church, and school curriculum.

The community has failed to use its power by demanding the home, churches, schools and government do more for these persons. Too often the community becomes disturbed by the crimes that are committed in their area and they want justice to be done right now. Yes, they want the offenders off the streets right now.

We are losing too many Blacks fathers, and Black boys to a system that is destroying the very existence of the Black race. Each year the crimes that are committed by Black men and Black boys are increasing by an alarming rate. All you have to do is watch your neighborhoods in order to see how many black boys and black men that are missing from your community as teachers in the schools systems, in your churches, social clubs, and government jobs and in other positions that Black men have held. The system is broken and it must be fixed before the Black race becomes an extinct race.

These gifted men and boys are capable of serving their government, family and community in a more productive way, if the system will change its judiciary direction of how Blacks are profiled and given maximum sentences in jails and in prisons. We must unite together as churches of all denominations of faith to save our race. There are some things we must do for ourselves. We as Blacks we should never forget where God has brought us from to where we are

PILLAR I: The Family

today. We are unlike like other races that help each other to stand on their feet when they are falling.

We see the circumstances that are taking place in our family and community where we live and turn our heads and look the other way and knowingly our family members or neighbors are having personal problems and want do nothing about it, only to say "they brought it on themselves," or, "They can get theirs just like I got mine."

It seems as if the governments on the local, state and federal levels are more concerned about keeping control of local communities by building prisons to take care of their financial needs of that community instead of helping young Black men learn how to get a good education. The government spends more money per year to keep a person in prison than its cost to send a person to college per year. In some data it has been reported that New York spends $180,000 per year on a person in prison and it costs $60,000 per year per student to attend one of their best universities. In another state it cost $80,000 per year to keep a person in prison per year, and it cost less than $40,000 per year to attend one of their colleges.

These gifted persons are trainable, and should enroll in a curriculum to receive instructional classes that will prepare them for the job market when they are released from prison. This will help them get a good education for the job markets when they are released from prison. Their training will help them readjust to their community by finding employment to support themselves, family and community by paying taxes to the government and restoring their family values.

Positive Parenting, School, Church and Community

Positive parenting, schools, churches and communities are the driving forces that help communities understand they are the driving forces that make positive changes.

When parents, schools, churches and community enter into an agreement that children are smart, intelligent, gifted, and beautiful, those children will gravitate to those words, and they will spend more time preparing their school work, by going to the library to live up to societies expectations . When children see role models they want to become, they will discipline themselves to reach their goals. When parents set goals which inspire, children can become leaders in their chosen field of study; and even the President of the United States! It's time for leaders of the family, school, church and community to come together to save their children by helping them whatever their needs may be. The first way to help is by listening to them.

Sometimes it may be just a pat on their backs, some words of encouraging, or a few extra dollars that will last a long time in their memories of years to come. Your children need your physical support in their school work, extra community activities: sports, drama, church activities, youth, choir, praise dance, and ushering. One of the best ways you can support them is to ask them how they are doing in their activities, and find out what their schedules are so that you can be there and support them and their team.

I have attended numerous school and church functions and didn't see that many parents or relatives present. When children see their parents and relatives in attendance it increases their awareness that their parents and relatives are supporting them. That gives them a sense of pride and the confidence to work that much harder to achieve their highest goals.

PILLAR I: The Family

Pastors in various congregations use the Sunday morning worship services to lift up their children's activities achievements: sports, academic grades and community involvements. This helps the children to understand that their pastor and congregation are with them. I have noticed how the children react when their names are called to come down to the front, they walk with pride and with confidence in themselves when the pastor states their achievements, and it makes them feel good. Their parents and the congregation share in their accomplishments and help foster a positive self-esteem. The children being featured develop a sense of self-worth.

PILLAR I: The Family

FAMILY WORKSHOPS

Cargle Family Reunion, Gary, IN 2011
(In front of the Jackson Five Family Home)

PILLAR I: The Family

In the Family Workshops that I have sponsored, many views and expressions have come from participants who were not honest in their ability to tell the truth. We set rules by asking all of the participants to share some of their experiences that they have had in married life. Some of the couples had been married for more than 10, 20, 30, 40 plus years, stated they had never had a cross word. One of the younger couple wanted to know how that could be. *You have been married for over forty years and you have never had a confrontation. How?* One of the brothers stated that is correct. He made a pledge when he got married he would not fight or argue with his wife over issues that were important to the family. If he and his wife were not able to discuss the issues, as Christians should, he would take a walk because he knew what augments would come to. After returning home most of the time the conversations will resume and the issues resolve themselves. Another couple responded by saying when their discussions begin to get out of hand the wife always chose to walk away. She stated that she has formed the opinion once her husband got started and wound up he can go on, and on, and on. Once she walks out and he sees that she has gone to the next room he will get louder and louder and that will go on for several minutes. She stated there is something about a person if you don't respond to them, they will not continue to fuss and fight with themselves because that would make them look crazy. After listening to others in the workshop they all agreed there must be a better way to handle husband and wife conflict other than abuse, fighting, name calling, acting like spoiled children, belittling each other, and talking about each other's families. God is not pleased when two grown people are acting out of control.

How to Resolve Conflict

> "And the Lord God formed man of the dust of the ground, and breathed into his nostrils the breath of life; and man became a living soul." Genesis 2:7

Men and Women were created by God. God made men to act differently because men are different. Men don't respond like women. And women don't respond like men. When we recognize our differences it helps us to learn to respect each other and make adjustments to understand where each other are coming from. We become more aware of what may trigger negative reactions in the first place. I think for me, knowing and accepting whatever each other's shortcoming or failures may be all you owe to each other. This knowledge will help you cease from trying to change one another. This knowledge allows you to help meet each other's basic needs through love and support.

My experiences have helped me to understand when you complement each other and help each other to meet their needs that will resolve some of the major stuff. Once the major stuff has been resolved stop washing each other's hands with the same old issues, singing the same old nagging song, repeating the same scripts over and over. For God blessings, before you start "Remember to say: I have been there and done that, and I am not going there anymore, so help me God!"

I have observed many happy married couples over the years. I asked one couple, Ben and Marsha, what it was that kept them happy together. Their answer was simple; paying attention to each other; knowing their needs and meeting their needs. "It is all in loving and sharing what you have," said Marsha. Ben agreed. "It may not be the big expenses, it may be just taking enough time to listen to your spouse, go out to breakfast, take in a movie, and spend some quality time in the bedroom nesting together with your partner." All of these suggestions will enhance your marriage into a new relationship that will add many more years of happiness.

As the twelfth child of my family, I can truthfully say I have never heard my mother and dad say foul words toward each other. How they did it is amazing to me. Twelve children to feed, clothe, discipline and provide for their spiritual and educational needs. It was God providing for all of our needs. However, I have seen my dad walk out of the house and keep himself busy around the house by doing repairs.

I remember an incident in the 40's, one of our neighbors ran a grocery store and the Sheriff raided his property searching for whisky and didn't find anything. The Sheriff came to our house and one of my sisters asked him if he had a Search Warrant. He told my sister, "Get out of the way girl before I push you out of the way!" When dad and mother returned home, dad was informed of what the sheriff had told my sister. That was the first time and the last time I heard dad use a curse word. Dad was so angry! The first thing dad did that Monday was to go to the Sheriff's office and the Sheriff apologized. He stated that someone had told them he was keeping whisky for the store owner.

Our parents had rules that were enforced at all time. They would every day remind us what those rules were. Did you do your homework on the inside and outside of the house? Taken care of feeding the animals, cleaning around the house and barn, did you take care of the inside of the house, making sure the kitchen and all rooms were in order, especially your clothes and school home works for the next day. In our home of the days were peace, respect, and Godly relationship between the children, mother, and father. Fighting and

PILLAR I: The Family
Family Workshops

cursing among brothers and sisters was not allowed in the home or the streets unless you were defending yourself.

Strong families are the foundations of churches, schools, community and government. When children come out of a God fearing home it denotes they have been instructed by parents and relatives who are committed and determined in helping their children to reach their highest achievements in the goals they seek. These parents are so very concerned that their children have active membership in churches, enrolled in character and culture building programs, such as Boys and Girls Club, Charm and Etiquette Clubs, Tots and Teens and other national enlightenment clubs. These are the type of families that build strong churches, schools, communities, and governments.

Marriage Is a Partnership

Marriage is a partnership, not a dictatorship.

> "Husbands, love your wives, even as Christ also loved the church, and gave himself for it;" Ephesians 5:25 *(KJSB)*

The marital responsibility of a husband to love his wife is outlined in this chapter. This denotes it is the responsibility of a husband to love his wife and protect her without receiving anything in return. As Christ gave himself for the church, so there is to be no sacrifice, not even the laying down of his life, that a husband is not a dictator; he is a leader and is expected to lead as God would have him to do.

However it is imperative that the husband understand where his wife is coming from when she raises questions on various subjects as it relates to love, sex, money, budget, household expenses, friends, sports, current events, in-laws and socializing.

PILLAR I: The Family
Family Workshops

Husbands must understand that a woman does not act and think like a man. He must listen to what she has to say and be willing to communicate by giving intelligent answers. He must understand that although he is the leader, he is not a dictator, and all major decisions must be understood and agreed upon by both before they are made. The husband is not to take the role he is the man of the house and what he says that's the way it is going to be. That's the way a dictator acts. Marriage is not a dictatorship, it's a partnership.

There must be togetherness; understanding what needs to be done and how soon it needs to be done. Too often husbands and wives think they can read each other's minds; this may be true in some instances. But never make a decision based upon assuming you are reading each other's minds. Marriages that are successful pay attention to their spouse. How are you going to reach their needs if you don't pay attention to what their needs are?

> "And the Lord God caused a deep sleep to fall upon Adam, and he slept: and he took one of his ribs, and closed up the flesh instead thereof; And the rib, which the Lord God had taken from man, made he a woman, and brought her unto the man." Genesis 2:21-22 (KJV)

Understand women don't think like men, and men don't think like women, but they all have certain needs. Men and women have spiritual needs, sexual needs and emotional needs. When these needs are met through the carious process of touching, kissing holding, hugging and sexual relationship all of our gifts that God put forth in his creation.

Yes, issues that cause misunderstandings come at a time in all of our lives. We need to repent, be calm and do what is right in the sight of God and ask for forgiveness and move on to the next day with God blessings. Don't forget your wedding vows;

PILLAR I: The Family
Family Workshops

always refer to the wedding vows. You are standing in the presence of God, as a servant of God in Jesus Christ.

Be careful what you are looking for, things that seem rosy may not be what God has for you. Little things matter; "Little things mean a lot" is a phrase that carry a lot of weight. Most husbands and wives can benefit from being reminded of this.

The following lists include some of those little things "Wives, particular, are usually deeply touched and encouraged through such things. And can be positively affected by little things from wives.

- Pray for your spouse daily.
- Tell your spouse that they are the greatest.
- Show them that you believe in them.
- Tell them daily that you love them.
- Hug often.
- Kiss tenderly and romantically at times.
- Show your partner that you enjoy talking about sex and meeting the other's needs.
- Show your commitment both privately and publicly.
- Show others that you are proud of your mate.
- Stress each other's strengths, not weaknesses.
- Stop trying to change him or her into somebody else.
- Show your spouse that you respect them more than anyone.
- Never give your spouse reason to doubt your love.
- Leave "I love you" notes in unexpected places.
- Let the other hear you thank God for him or her.
- Hold each other's hands while walking or sitting.
- Always sit by each other when possible.
- Men, always open the doors for your woman.
- Men, take her flowers unexpectedly.
- Men, plan a surprise night out.
- Men, call during the day to just say "I love you."
- Men, always call and tell her if you will be late.
- Men, let your woman find you staring lovingly at her.

PILLAR I: The Family
Family Workshops

Marriage needs to be built on God's foundation truths, the marriages relationship should bless each partner, and specific responsibilities should be delegated to each partner; Communication is one of the important building blocks of a strong marriage; And "little things mean a lot."

The late Jerry Solomon, former Director of Field Ministries and Mind Games Coordinator for Probe Ministries, advises us to be specialists when dating; always be nice, respectful, loving, treating you like a queen or king, and show respect for family members.

How do they share what they have? Are they respectful? Do they come on time? Are they always late driving a dirty car, not clean, and always broke when they show up? One of the best ways to make sure this person has what you are looking for is to pay attention to their job profession, education, respect, integrity as a Christian, kind heart, love for their mother and father and relatives, dress attire and how they show love for you.

PILLAR I: The Family
Family Workshops

Marriage Takes Three
Marriage takes three to be complete;
It's not enough for two to meet.
They must be united in love
By love's Creator, God above.
Then their love will be firm and strong;
Able to last when Things go wrong,
Because they've felt God's love and know
He's always there, He'll never go.

And they have both loved Him in kind
With all the heart and soul and mind,
And in that love they've found the way
To love each other every day.

A marriage that Follows God's plan
Takes more than a woman and a man.
It needs a oneness that can be
Only from Christ -
Marriage takes three.
(*Beth Stuckwisch*)

Practice What You Teach Your Children

As parents, we instilled in our children they had to go to Sunday school, Christian Youth Fellowship (CYF), Sunday worship services, and all activities pertaining to them. Our children were allowed to go to social functions and they were informed, by us, what goes on at parties. We explained to them that some children smoke, drink, use drugs, and are involved in sexual activities. They were instructed to call if the party got out of hand. At our house, we had recreational equipment in the lower level, books and magazine for children to read and snacks to eat. Our children were free to invite their friends to the house, just as their friends invited them.

We discussed in our family sessions church work, school work, tithing, budgeting, homework, your goals in life, how to

PILLAR I: The Family
Family Workshops

relate to your friends, and the type of people you form a relationship with. You must watch their attitudes, how they talk and their attitudes with their family in their homes. What are their life goals? Where do they work and what are their professional goals? How well are they doing in schools? Are they involved in school activities, are they on the honor role? Do they apply themselves to obtain the maximum from their education studies, and goals they are working toward?

One of the areas parents must teach their children is budgeting and the cost of operating a home. The general expenses: repairs, insurance, utilities, mortgage, property and lawn services. These are some of the basics that all families should be knowledgeable in teaching their children sound budgeting.

All children are different, and all children have the genes of their parents to make their personalities. Too often we look at our children and see ourselves, as parents working in their personalities. We see us in their talking mannerisms, communications, friendliness, smarts, behaviors, anxiety, anger; how they express themselves through leadership, or if they are standoffish, and want to be alone reading or writing. There is nothing wrong when there are healthy signs of both parents producing strong healthy bodies that are mentally, educationally, spiritually and morally present in the lives of children when they are growing and become mature adults. However, if you see or observe some signs that are not taking place in your child's growth, you need to seek professional help immediately. It's better to seek help at an early stage than wait until the child enrolls in school.

These are the basic institutions that makes things happened in all communities. Where there are strong families who have trained their children and their children have trained their

PILLAR I: The Family
Family Workshops

children in the word of God, the value of getting a good education, and knowing how to get along with people.

During my life time I have been involved in many sessions with parents and their children regarding conflicts. Most of the sessions are like this, "My children just don't respect me, nor do they respect the rules of the family." What are the rules? I ask. Simple, "Clean up your room, wash the dishes, get your homework done, go to school on time, stay off the telephone, don't watch too much TV, make sure you are home before curfew, and don't get involved with the wrong group."

Remember Proverbs 22:6, "Train a child in the way he should go, and when he is old he will not depart from it." As parents, you have the responsibility to set the guidelines and boundaries for your child's future. As a mother and father, make sure your child understands each rule and help them to understand if they are not followed they have to pay the cost. God expects you, the mother and the father, to enforce the rules to establish regulations and impose the punishment when rules are broken. I know there are homes where there are rebellious children who have no respect for anyone, all because the rules and regulations were not enforced and no punishment for rule breaking was given.

Most of all parenting experts agree that children need firm, clear boundaries in order to learn appropriate behavior and to grow into reasonable, responsible adults. Very few parents would disagree, at least in theory. So why so much difficulty setting limits and saying no to their children?

Here Are Some of the Reasons:
- We want to keep their friendship
- We want to avoid conflict
- We want to keep peace in the family
- We feel guilty when saying no

PILLAR I: The Family
Family Workshops

- We fear what may happen if we say no
- We don't want to be like our own parents. Those who were raised in very strict home may feel strongly that "I am not going to be like my parents."
- We don't want our children to go through what we went through.

Saying "No" Is Positive Parenting. When children are babies, you first say no to protect them from danger. As they begin to grow and explore, you must teach them not to touch the hot stove or climb up where they can hurt themselves. As children get older the stakes get higher, and higher.

All too soon, your children will be confronting issues: SAT tests, graduating from high school, choosing college, choosing a professional career, falling in love. From a negative side: learning to stay away from drugs, drinking, peer pressure, sex, and dating. Associating with the wrong group may pull them from their educational pursuit, and church involvement. Parenting is a 24-hour-7-day a week vocation. You never finished you just let up for a while to observe their actions of what they are into. Some parents' eyes and ears are trained to see and hear all of the mistakes their children make, but never see or hear any positive things they do. Parent should not spend all of their valuable time on being critical of their children for what they are not doing, finding faults, and negating.

Instead, praise your children when they have done a superb work in their school, home chores and other activities that deserve accommodation. Your teen agers will have to make choices that affect their safety and well-being as they navigate these difficult, confusing years, the best protection they can have is God and their own judgment. The firm, caring guidance you provide as they grow is by saying no to bad behavior and saying yes to good behavior. These acts of

PILLAR I: The Family
Family Workshops

praise will help cultivate their good judgment and provide a model for making smart choices. The family, I often think of what Paul said in his writing in the Epistle to the Colossians "The Church that is in your house."

Religion moves in different areas and organizes itself around different centers. There is personal religion, which we carry around with us and live by the inner regions of our personalities. There is ecclesiastical religion, institutionalized in churches, with their traditions, polities, rituals, and rubrics. And there is family religion which, when it is at its best, floods with light and makes the relationships therein sacred and beautiful. It creates a church within a house. We are concerned with this last area of religious life.

Religion when it is practiced has a great impact upon the home, church, school, community and government. The home is the most powerful learning center in God's creation. It is where we learn the basic skills of communicating what we learn, and sharing those ideas as we form relationships in the home, with the school, with the church and with the community. Without a strong foundation that comes from the home, our schools, churches and communities will not become institutions as productive as they should be. What comes out of the homes will show up in these places. What happens to one inevitably happens to the other.

The family is at the center of maintaining productive churches, schools, and communities. If the family life of this nation becomes nonproductive what will our institutions become? From what I have observed over the years as a pastor and a Presiding Elder, many of the churches and denominations are not maintaining growth in membership. Sunday Schools, children, youth and adult ministries are not as it were twenty five or forty years ago. It's alarming to see crises that are taken place in families today: broken homes,

PILLAR I: The Family
Family Workshops

broken relationships, homes without fathers, or mothers struggling to provide for her children.

We came from homes and we live in homes now, where our deepest personal interests are more important to us than in the problems of our family. And when we step outside our individual concerns and consider the nation, it grows daily more obvious that the real battle ground for the moral life of America in the family. We may multiply our inventions and rise to its pinnacle of highly articulated, mechanized miracle of a civilization which we have started here. We may increase our industries and accumulate wealth. We may even build great temples dedicated to public worship and great schools dedicated to public education. But after all, what this country will amount to in the end depends upon what happens in its homes. There is no substitute for parents.

PILLAR II: THE SCHOOL

PILLAR II: The School

I am Dr. Sharon Johnson-Shirley, Superintendent of Lake Ridge New Tech Schools. I have been an educator for over thirty years. I have served in various capacities such as teacher, principal, curriculum director, assistant superintendent and ten years as superintendent. In my opinion it is safe to assume that I write with expert knowledge. I am honored that Rev. Carrell K. Cargle, Sr. has invited me to discuss in his book information that I have observed over the years as an educator and make suggestions for the future.

Before I begin, I would like to thank Rev. Cargle for having the foresight to write a book that sheds light on the ills of society that cause the breakdown of the family unit. I also would like to thank him for having the fortitude to make suggestions on how we all can make improvements in our lives that will lead to a better world if we just work together. Rev. Cargle has been very instrumental in my life for many years and for that, my life is better. His continuous support, many days of prayer, and being there for me even when I do not call has helped me to become the person and leader that I am today.

In this segment, I would like to discuss: How raising children in the home impacts how children behave in school. Parents are the first teacher. They teach children from the womb to school, and that sets the tone for their offspring to be successful or become failures. I will approach the conversation from families and schools in urban districts. I would like to add a disclaimer. "This is not a one size fits all discussion. There are exceptions to all rules."

In a large number of urban homes often times there is disconnect within families due to poverty. Parents are often maintaining two or more jobs to make ends meet. Therefore, children are raising themselves and sometimes their younger siblings. Generational poverty exists and finds that in a lot of cases great-grand parents and grandparents are still the glue that keeps the family unit together. They are the immediate parent that children will interact with daily. However, this places an undue burden on those family members because they are in their golden years, have raised their children and deserve an opportunity to rest. In some cases parents disregard their responsibilities by placing the task of raising their children solely on their parents.

PILLAR II: The School

Sometimes, this task does not even come with monetary support. Also, single parent homes and foster parents create another family dynamic that impacts the way students interact in school. We also are seeing more evidence of homeless families and abused children. In some of these cases we are blessed that the child makes it to school at all. Often times, teachers do not have the cultural training to understand why the student is having problems or cannot make it to school on time. Instead of dealing with the problem later after class, teachers will often create more problems for the student by confronting the child in front of the entire class. This embarrasses the child and sometimes the child shuts down. Educators expect them to learn and be at their best behavior in spite of the circumstances.

Parents send us the best children they have and they utilize the best skills they have in raising children. An old cliché says, "Children were not born with an instruction book." In addition, the expectations of schools are far greater that just educating the student. The role of schools has changed tremendously. Because of the mandates, accountability, and the needs of students, educators are leaving the profession or not entering it at all. If the government does not find the money to pay teachers and administrators, the educational field is going to find a shortage in highly qualified educators.

Social media plays a major role in attitudes and behavior; and is both a negative and positive influence on students. Children are sitting on couches without exercising or playing with other children. They are not creating or building relationships with people. They have their own world.

When they come to school they want to be entertained. If they are not entertained they are bored. Motivation and effort are lacking. When using social media in a positive way and monitored, students can become innovators, and can create relationships globally. There are many activities on the internet that can lead to positive academic and social success, but adults need to model and teach students ways to be problem solvers, innovators and how to use social media productively and safely.

Often educators will describe parents not being involved in school activities that help to create a partnership between school and home. Research has proven time and time again that when parents are involved in school activities students tend to be more engaged. When you talk about parent involvement schools must do a better job in teaching parents what involvement means. Some activities that are simple and should be shared with parents are as simple as talking with their children about the school day, and recognizing that students have feelings. Sometimes children just want to be heard and recognized. Educators need to do a better job in welcoming parents into the schools and recognizing that they too may need help.

Another suggestion for parents is to make sure that their children know that they as parents are concerned and care about their child's school day activities as well as their safety. Getting up with their children in the mornings just to know how they were dressed when they left home for school. Questions that need to be answered include: Were the children dressed properly for the weather? Are they safe standing on the bus line? Were they in compliance with school dress codes and appropriateness?

Parents need to check in with teachers often to find out how their child is doing. Most times parents visit schools when schools call them with a problem. When the child knows that parents are in contact with the school and that school is in partnership with the parents for the success of the student, students' behavior tend to be better and grades improve. We must have two way communications from school to home and home to school.

Sometimes educators assume that they know all of the needs of the students, parents and families, but usually until faced with a crisis they do not know the underlying factors of the family situation that is impacting the student at school. Educators must create a trust factor so that parents will reach out for help. This will lead to a better understanding of the child's needs.

In summary, working together we all can improve society and produce students that are capable of leading the world.

Dr. Sharon Johnson-Shirley

PILLAR II: The School

The Importance of Schools in Communities

It is imperative that all family members be embraced by loving schools and congregations who are committed to reaching the needs of everyone. These needs are met by the ministries that are offered in the Family Workshops. The church's teaching helps all families reach higher levels in all of their needs and aspirations.

The major concerns of Black families and their communities are jobs, good schools, family crises, housing, lack of strong male images of leadership, crime, school dropouts, and lack of police protection. Families want a safe community for children, young adults and senior citizens; and they want venues for positive things to do. The questions raised by parents are: *Will my child be able to graduate from high school and college in the community we are living without worry of the killings and dropouts*? The questions raised by their children are the same: *Will I be able to graduate from high school and college in the community where I am living without worry of gang violence and negative peer pressure*?

I talked to a group of students during their six weeks summer program at Allen Metropolitan C.M.E. Church in Chicago, where the Rev. Dr. David L. Bryant, Jr. is the pastor. Their most important concerns were: their goals, finding a job after graduating from high school and college; college relationships, academic security such as scholarships for college, and a job after graduating. They wanted to be successful in reaching their goals and become productive citizens.

Many of our children are enrolled in colleges and universities because this is what mother and father wanted, and not what they wanted. The questions in many families today should be, *are my children ready to go to college?* The concerns should be *do they really know what they want to major in? Do they have the guidance counselors and parents understanding and support for what they want to major in? Are they mature enough to go out on their own? Can they make wise and mature decisions when pressure and demands are placed on them?* These are profound questions that most parents should work on from grades K thru12.

Parents have a duty to make sure their children have an outstanding academic work ethic that will enable them to be successful throughout their academic career. One way is by instilling consistent study practices so that they learn to study independently.

Children must understand they have to be just as committed to their academic subjects as they are to sports and non-academic subjects. They ought to be more committed to their major courses than attending parties are going to sports events.

We must train our children how to be responsible, honest, respectful and understanding. We must encourage them to have loving relationships with their parents, pastors, church family, teachers, counselors, peers and significant people in their lives. We owe it to them to lead them through their education process and enable them to move successfully from one stage to another in order to reach their professional goals in life. We as parents, educators and the church need to plant seeds and put structures in place to insure that our children will rise to the best of their possibilities, and not become tragic statistics of a generation that did not fulfill their potential.

How Do You Handle Problems?
The family, school, and church are the institutions that are responsible for whatever happens in a community, for good or bad. From the family comes children who are loved,

PILLAR II: The School

molded into persons to be taught as they enter into the school as students to learn from the curriculum that have been provided to reach children's need.

Schools, along with families and churches, are leading institutions that ought to should be teaching responsibilities, relationships, stewardship, citizenship, education, and respect for people and properties. There seems to be a lack of togetherness from the leadership of Black churches and communities to unify their efforts and develop a blue print to help Black communities overcome their ills. This is needed in order to become productive citizens to counteract the forces that are destroying inner cities schools, businesses and communities.

These are some of the major issues that are not being implemented through a consorted effort by families, schools and churches located in communities where there seems to be a lack of support from their people. Just look around churches in the urban areas, and you will see communities that are neglected. Negative attitudes of citizens reflect a lack of education, disconnected family structure, broken family relationships, teenage pregnancies, incarcerated fathers, lack of jobs, or religious educational teaching that comes from structured programs, geared to overcoming poverty, crimes, and restoring their communities.

All of these illnesses are the source of a community that is declining. It shows communities that have schools and churches built throughout their neighborhoods that are not reaching the needs of God's people. It is now time for all religious leaders and their institutions to come together with educational leaders to assess the needs of their communities and develop a strategic plan to overcome the problems that are destroying communities.

PILLAR II: The School

The leaders need to do a better job working together to reach those persons who are dropouts of schools, dropouts of churches, members of gangs and those participating in crime activities that have caused so many communities to become what they are today. They become communities that are poverty stricken, without jobs and access to health care.

Schools and churches need to prepare men, women and children who are committed and willing to give their time and efforts of reaching people who are waiting for their lives to be transformed. The teachings in schools and churches ought to help all people understand the saving power of a good education. Education will save individuals, families and community from becoming victims of hopelessness.

Schools and churches should be out front promoting objectives and goals that are related to family life, education, jobs, citizenship, health, and moral values. These institutions should help implement programs that are good for its people, such as job security. By helping the unemployed and the underemployed secure jobs, they keep their properties, their communities clean, and offer a safe haven for children. Healthy families yield zero tolerance for crime, prevent school dropouts and poverty. What a beautiful sight it will be to see families, school, churches and communities working together to overcome issues that have plagued and negatively impacted our communities!

People are calling for the leadership in their communities to come forward and speak words of encouragement. People that have become involved in church fellowships are able to draw other persons into relationships which form cluster services for people who desire to work together, in order to improve their neighborhoods and communities.

PILLAR II: The School

I believe when families, schools, churches and communities do come together acting on one accord and the people of God see togetherness, it sends a powerful message throughout the community.

One way of doing this is to have Church and school names placed strategically throughout the community denoting they are working on one accord to improve family life: educationally, physically, spiritually, morally, and financially. This form of branding can be very effective.

This effort will enable the citizens who live in those communities and outsiders to see and feel the presence of those churches and schools showing their togetherness and partnerships to overcome whatever the situations may be. *Together We Stand, Divided We Fall.* Look around your community, what do you see? Do you see problems? Do you see communities not together? Do you see families not together? Do you see political parties not together; Black leaderships not together? You see city halls across the country not together! You see school boards not together! You see county government not together! You see state houses across the country not together! You see the White House and Congress not together! *"Together We Stand, Divided We Fall."*

Together we stand, because we see the needs and the willingness of the spirit that bring us to the table, enabling us to work together to accomplish the needed goals that are before us. Look around you, we have created too many issues have allowed us to divide families, communities, School Boards, City halls, County governments, State houses, Church houses and the White House. When leaders are divided it hurts the citizens who are in need the most: Those who are poverty stricken, sick and lacking health insurance, food and a safe environment, and police protection. Those who have no voice to be heard have created many downfalls in communities.

The leadership of schools and churches must become the voices that fall upon the communities and be led out of the situation they find themselves in. Hosea 4:6 reads, "My people are destroyed from lack of knowledge, because you have rejected knowledge."

Hosea was confronted by religious leaders of Jeroboam 1 who rebelled against Solomon's son Rehoboam. Many issues confronted him daily as he assumed the leadership role over the Northern Kingdom of Israel. God selected Hosea, because of his commitment to Him, his love for the people and his many problems with his family and adulterous wife. Political and religious leaders rebelled against him for his teaching, against sinful life styles that were practiced by the citizens and priests who were unwilling to accept God's teaching. These leaders chose to accept the teaching of a rival kingdom in the north and established their own religious system in violation of God's law, and made two golden calves and ordered the people to worship them instead of God.

Rehoboam also appointed his own priests, who were descendants of Aaron. At first the residents of the northern kingdom continued to worship God, even though they were doing it in the wrong way. Very soon they also began to worship Canaanite gods. Before long they had substituted Baal for God and no longer worshiped God at all. Man's first response to God was to live. We cannot help to observe the message within the concept; man was expected to live for God. This accounting helps us to understand, man has a desire to create systems which perhaps replace God and eliminate principles established by God for His created. Can it be said; we too, are very far from God?

Dropout Prevention – Teach Me Who I am

In my pastoral duties as a clergyman, parent, and One Church One School (OCOS) activist, I have seen the negative impacts that come from children who were trapped in homes where negative parenting practices were the rule of the day. These practices have contributed to so many behavioral problems in the lives of their children as they enter schools, churches and other public places. Every year, close to one third of these students, within the eighteen year old age range does not finish high school. The dropout rates for minority students, students from low income families, and disabled students are even higher. This is not just a problem affecting certain individuals and schools; it is a community wide problem that affects everyone. High school dropouts commit about 75 percent of crimes in the United States and are much more likely to be on public assistance than those who complete high school.

The cost to the public for those crimes and welfare benefits is close to $200 billion annually. Dropouts earn only about 40 percent of the income of college degree holders, resulting in about $50 billion dollars in lost state and federal tax revenues each year. For decades, educators have labored to help these kids, but a community wide problem needs a community wide solution. Moreover, schools *want* community help.

A survey conducted by the Pew Partnership for Civic Change in 2003 found that 93 percent of literacy workers said they could use more volunteers to help people learn to read. 75 percent of public educators said they could use more volunteers to work in classrooms, and 60 percent of teachers said they could use more people to assist with the collection of donated books and other school supplies. The demand for help is as great as the scope of the problem. What can the communities do to help stem this tide?

PILLAR II: The School

What Dropouts Say

In order for the community to intervene and help dropouts, community members must know what dropouts themselves, think about their situation. Civic Enterprises recently interviewed dropouts and asked them what they thought would improve their ability to finish school, and also asked the community what would improve a potential dropout's chance for staying in school.

Dropouts said that the following could help them:
- *Improve teaching and curricula to enhance the connection between school and work. 81% of dropouts said there should be more opportunities for "real world" learning so that students can see the connection between school and getting a job. (Civic Enterprises 2002)
- *Improve access to support for struggling students. 81% of dropouts surveyed wanted "better" teachers. 75% wanted smaller classes. 70% believed that more tutoring, summer school and extra time with teachers would have improved their chances of graduating. (Civic Enterprises 2006)
- *Foster academics. 70% of dropouts said that "increasing supervision in school" and 62% said "more classroom discipline" was necessary to ensure success. 57% said that their schools" did not do enough to help students feel safe from violence. (Civic Enterprises 2006)
- *Promote close relationships with adults. Only 41% of dropouts reported having someone to talk to about personal problems. 62% said they would like to see schools do more to help students with problems outside of class. Only 47% said the schools even bothered to contact them after they dropped out. (Civic Enterprises 2006)

PILLAR II: The School

Factors that lead to dropping out:
If community members are to get involved in the dropout problem, they should be aware of the kinds of factors that place with children at risk of dropping out. BYTTF – Boston Youth Transitions Task Force's research findings based on surveys, interviews and focus groups with Boston area students, parents, teachers and youth service providers show that many factors are at work in the decision to drop out:

- The relationship between students and teachers is the most important factor in student's school experience, whether positive or negative. (BYTTF 2006)
- The disruptiveness of peers in school causes students to feel distracted and unsafe, leading to increased chance of dropping out. (BYTTF 2006)
- The pace of instruction is an important reason youth give for leaving school. Students who need extra attention and don't receive it are likely to dropout.(BYTTF 2006)
- Personal problems cause youth to leave school if they do not have a trusted adult from whom they can seek help. (BYTTF 2006)
- Students in small alternative programs appreciate the increased attention and the opportunity to work at their own pace. (BYTTF 2006)
- Weak academic skills can cripple efforts to recover dropouts in "second chance" programs unless they receive even more attention from community volunteers. (BYTTF 2006)
- Economic needs can compete with pursuing education after dropping out.(BYTTF 2006)
- Students who come from single parent families, have a mother who dropped out of high school, have parents who provide low support for learning, or have parents who do not know their friends' parents well are also all at a higher risk of dropping out than

PILLAR II: The School

other students. (BYTTF 2006) Healthy Families & Children 11 Facts About High School

Dropout Rates
1. Every year, over 1.2 million students drop out of high school in the United States alone. That's a student every 26 seconds or 7,000 a day.
2. About 25% of high school freshmen fail to graduate from high school on time.
3. The U.S., which had some of the highest graduation rates of any developed country, now ranks 22nd out of 27 developed countries.
4. The dropout rate has fallen 3% from 1990 to 2010 (12.1% to 7.4%)
5. The percentage of graduating Latino students has significantly increased. In 2010, 71.4% received their diploma vs 61.4% in 2006. However, Asian American and white students are still far more likely to graduate than Latino and African American students.
6. A high school dropout will earn $200.000 less than a high school graduate over his lifetime. And almost a million dollars less than a college graduate.
7. In 2010, 38 states had higher graduation rates. Vermont had the highest rate, with 91.4% graduating. And Nevada had the lowest with 57.8% of students graduating.
8. Almost 2,000 high schools across the U.S. graduate less than 60% of their students.
9. These "dropout factories" account for over 50% of the students who leave school every year.
10. 1 in 6 students attends a *dropout factory* (a high school having a high proportion of students who drop out before completing their course of study.) 1 in 3 minority students (32%) attend a dropout factory, compared to 8% of white students.

PILLAR II: The School

11. In the U.S., high school dropouts commit 75% of crimes. Black men lag behind their peers in other races when it comes to graduating from both two and four year colleges, according to federal statistics that track their completion through 2009 2012, respectively. (Sources: 11 facts About High School Dropout Rates/DoSomething.org. Dropout Rates among Minority Men in Colleges)

Only a third of Black male students graduate from four year colleges within six years, compared with 45 percent of Hispanic men, 57 percent of white men, and 64 percent of Asian men. Graduation rates within in 6 years, graduating from both two and four year colleges: 21 33% of Black Males, 45% of Hispanic Males, 57% of White Males, 64% of Asian males. The report makes 11 policy recommendations aimed at better preparing and tracking students as they progress from kindergarten through 12th grade.

In addition, it offers four rationales that specifically relate to higher education. First, establish early alert systems for all Title IV degree granting colleges. A student who missed several classes in a row early in the semester might receive an electronic message directing him to a counselor or adviser. If he ignored the message, his phone would ring. The adviser would help identify academic or personal roadblocks and would steer him to services that could help.

"There are so many interventions, including counseling and tutoring, that could be put in place that we know work, but by the time students are referred, it's too late, and they've fallen through the cracks," J. Luke Wood, co-director of the Minority Male Community College Collaborative at San Diego State University said in an interview with the Chronicle of Higher Education. (*U.S. Is Urged to Curtail Alarming Dropout Rates Among Minority Men* Katherine Mangan, 2014) There is no

PILLAR II: The School

reason why parents and citizens should not become involved with the schools systems and colleges to formulate a working plan to decrease the number of students who are dropping out of schools and colleges. This information should enable the public to scrutinize, analyze and discipline information intelligently without been misled."

In the 2014 report, *Advancing the Success of Boys and Men of Color in Education,* it stated that "colleges that are already required by federal law to disclose completion and graduation rates should break those down by race or ethnicity and by gender within those groups. That would provide 'a more nuanced understanding of how colleges and universities foster differential outcomes by student backgrounds."

The Leadership Council of Parents and the administration of schools and colleges needs to help the public to get a better understanding of what needs to be done to improve the achievement of those students who are having problems. The public should not be ignorant or misinformed on subjects that are before the school board and college requirements. As citizens you must fight for your schools, city and county government, state and federal government. It is your responsibility to be a voice in your school, communities, city, state, federal levels and town hall meetings. As parents and family members you owe it to your children and community to make your voices heard for changes that are needed to make progress.

You do this by making your voices heard in school board meetings, visiting your child's school and observing what is taking place at the school, on the playground, and in the classroom. You need to know your child's teacher's name, who is the guidance counselor, have a relationship with the school's principal and investigate the curriculum being

PILLAR II: The School

offered in the school. When parents lose interest and show no concern, chances are the school administration, and teachers will gradually lose interest in the children they are teaching. As parents and concerned citizens, we must accept some of the responsibility for inadequate schools and social programs.

Too many children are failing in schools and we need to take a look at why this is happening. So many of our children are not graduating from high school! Why is the dropout rate so high in the Black Community? Why are so many of the teachers losing interest in educating Black children? Why are curriculums not designed to warn parents and students before dropouts occur? Why is it that the school curriculum is not offering classes that provide jobs for students when they are potential dropouts? Why have so many Black students become chronic absentees from school?

Willie Williams, author of the Black Male College Experience says the system is stacked against black males. He was enrolled as a student in the Education Department at a prestigious university in Chicago. He records being the only black male within the department. On graduation day, Mr. Williams discovered he was one of two black males participating in graduation that day. How can this be? Surely this failure rests upon many shoulders. Black males are not failing. Institutions are failing them.

PILLAR II: The School

One Church One School Resolution read at General Conference1994 (Dr. Phedonia Johnson, Mrs. Ester Isom, Dr. Doris Williamson, Bishop Henry M. Williamson)

One Church One School Educational Ministry

As one of the founders of the **One Church One School (OCOS) Educational Ministry,** God inspired me to draft a Resolution for the 1994 General Conference that the One Church One School become a national organization that all Episcopal districts in the connectional adapt a school in their community and urge all faith based denominations to become involved in the OCOS National Organization. The General Conference of 1994 voted to adapt the resolution. This resolution was discussed with Rev. Dr. Henry M. Williamson, Sr., founder of the OCOS, and Dr. Phendonia Johnson, National Education Director. Dr Johnson read the Resolution and made a motion, and the rest is history.

The founder of One Church One School, Bishop Henry M. Williamson, saw the need for such a movement with the church as the connector or bridge for home and school relationships. As stated by Bishop Williamson: The "P"

PILLAR II: The School

Principle: Pastors, Popular Personalities, Policemen, Professionals, Politicians, Philanthropists, Press, Parents, Pupils, and Principals empowering one another for the betterment of community. Now more than ever, we must join together to strengthen and fortify them for our global society. One Church One School is built upon the foundation n described by the African Proverb: *"It takes a whole village to raise a child."*

Educating our children is a part of our village responsibility. The church and school must be committed to and dedicated to a single vision of this shared responsibility. Williamson believes that teaching The Value of Life and the Value of Learning, to our children in the One Church One School Partnership Program will foster excellence and accomplishments in the future. This is a movement that we as leaders must nurture and reinforce in a race against evils that reach out for control of the minds and spirits our children.

Our ancestors have given us a legacy of excellence and accomplishments. Now it is incumbent upon us to do all that is necessary to pass the torch of excellence to our descendants, so that they may achieve their hopes and dreams." Williamson went on to say, "I know that utilizing the "P' Principle to teach The Value Of Life Of Learning, to our children in the One Church One School Partnership Program will serve as a foundation for success in the present. Full participation in OCOS is essential if it is to become a viable and influential movement. It is my hope that each church will be involved in a church/school partnership."

PILLAR II: The School

Brief History of One Church One School

The Christian Methodist Episcopal Church (CME) has a unique and long history of partnership between church and school. CME origin is rooted in the connection between church and school. Its mission has not changed from Reading, Race and Religion, the "Three R's" for the CME in the 19th century to its historical colleges and One Church One School: "Teaching the Value of Life and the Value of Learning in the 21st century."

Significantly, some of the same academic, personal and social needs of our people that faced our forefathers have emerged today. Under the leadership of Bishop Henry M. Williamson, Sr. and the College of Bishops developed OCOS out of the CME history as an outreach ministry to meet the academic, social and personal needs of young people, their families, and communities. The CME OCOS partnerships have acted as a catalyst in their respective communities and inspired churches of varied denominations to join them in this strategy to save our children.

PILLAR II: The School

The Vision
The vision of One Church One School is that every school in our nation will be in partnership with one or more neighboring churches to improve the achievement, social behavior and personal development of our children and youth.

Goals
- Every church and every school in a partnership
- A cadre of trained church/school volunteers in every OCOS partnership
- Every child in every partnership values life and values learning
- Nationwide school district implementation of OCOS partnerships
- Improve academic achievement, social behavior and personal development for each child in an OCOS partnership

Strategy
Today this national network of OCOS partnerships include: after school and in school programs, homework centers, tutoring and mentoring programs, nursery schools for children of teenage mothers, summer educational and recreational and attendance programs. Also included are the Dr. Martin Luther King, Jr. Dream Keepers Workshops, Freedom Schools programs, Student Empowerment Seminars, parent safety patrols, and many more supportive child-centered programs.

Each year, a national partnership conference is held the third Friday in October where participants come from all over the country to learn more about church/school partnerships, for volunteer training, networking, the creation of new partnerships and strengthening of existing ones.

PILLAR II: The School

Future
One Church One School welcomes new partnerships to the national network and looks forward to the involvement of an international community in the future. One Church One School, a Community Partnership Program, is headquartered at 7841 South Wabash Avenue, Chicago, IL, 60619.
For more information, visit:
http://www.onechurchoneschool.org/

PILLAR III: THE CHURCH

PILLAR III: The Church

What Are We Preaching? What Are We Teaching?

In many church communities, leaders of Faith Based Organizations are teaching what several persons have deemed as a "Self-Centered Theology." The fundamental premise of this teaching requires persons to base their ability to achieve upon themselves. Followers of this teaching are taught to attribute their measure of success on the popularity afforded to them within their circle of influence. Believers are motivated to seek answers for life's issues by looking or seeking for the God within themselves. By doing so, they are able to acquire the blessings of life by believing what will ultimately become their reality.

These teachings are in opposition to the teachings of Christ. Christology requires one to consider the needs of others. Jesus taught and modeled the Kingdom of God is great and available to man through commonalities. As we move away from the teachings of the Lord Jesus Christ and the Word of God becomes re-interpreted, I believe today just as it was in Biblical times, there are church leaders who God is accusing of destroying the lives of people.

God's displeasure is not expressed through the plagues of old but is evidenced through the decline of social and moral fabrics. As individuals seek to live as they please, societal norms become more skewed. Modern man lacks knowledge of bible based teaching and these principles currently seem undesirable and restrictive. People seem to be lacking knowledge and understanding because a great number of them appear to be less able to search the word of God's biblical truths for themselves. They would rather be told what is correct instead of reading what has been recorded as correct modes of living.

Too often we hear church folks say, "If the preacher said it was right, then, it must be alright."

PILLAR III: The Church

And if my pastor tells me that such and such is alright, then, what I am doing must be alright. If the bishop does it, the pastors do it, the prophets do it, the deacons, and the missionaries are doing it, so it must be alright to follow the example set before me. Church leaders have an awesome responsibility of teaching what is right and what is wrong. Spiritual leaders must be prepared for the race before them at all times. There's not but one way, and that's the way of Christ! Pray Up! Stay Up! And be filled with the Holy Spirit! Spiritual leadership is a heavy responsibility for bishops, elders, priests, teachers, judges, missionaries, counselors and believers. Those walking and witnessing daily within their circle of influence have a charge to keep.

As leaders, we are responsible for leading people to higher grounds. We are responsible for helping persons to overcome their fears and insecurities about others and themselves. With the development of confidence and faith, comes the ability which enables people to contribute to their community and society. The causes of many of the problems we are having in all communities are rooted perhaps in these: 1) the lack of knowledge, and 2) the desire to be a risk taker. Our problems do not stem from a shortage of information, but rather from people rejecting creditable information.

Every time I enter a city and drive through a community, I notice the surroundings. A person can tell a lot about a community by noticing if trash and other items are blowing on the streets. The character of a neighborhood can be determined by noticing how well sidewalks, lawns, and parkways are being maintained. Does the neighborhood express beauty through its planting of trees and flowers? Have officials cared for streets by removing pot holes, provided for safety via traffic signs and signals? Is there appropriate city lighting? And how well are buildings maintained throughout the community?

PILLAR III: The Church

My vision also pulls me towards the attractive sights of the neighborhoods, and I wonder why the total neighborhood is not a source of visually beautiful things. Hosea in his profound teaching was correct when he said: "My people are destroyed for a lack of knowledge: because thou hast rejected knowledge, I will also reject thee." I often say to myself, "What a shame this neighborhood has become." Who is to blame for the shame on these neighborhoods? Does blame fall at the feet of the religious leaders, family members, elected officials, business owners, and teachers? Is it the police officers, judges, court system? Is it the children who play in the street, or the drivers and passengers in automobiles that dispose their garbage anywhere and any place? What about poverty, crimes, gang elements, or property owners who do not pay their taxes?

Hosea was right when he said my people are destroyed for lack of knowledge. Because they have rejected knowledge and disobeyed the teaching of God's words and have forgotten the foundation of their parents and reject the teachings of civic pride from their parents, teachers, pastors, schools and churches.

What is the Church?

The Church is the Lord's House and has been consecrated for public worship for those who are Christians, and for those who desire to become a Christian. A building set apart for God's people as a denomination of believers to come together and worship. The Church is a fellowship of believers, with ministries that move beyond the walls of a church building, to meet the needs of God's people, by providing spiritual, physical, mental, educational, social and benevolent services designed to reach the needs of the people of God, and to evangelize them into the fellowship of believers of the local congregation.

PILLAR III: The Church

In the process of reaching people throughout the community from all walks of life, the church must be mindful to the needs of the family; their homes, their schools, and their communities. This includes church hoppers and dropouts. The Church, through its ministries must have the leadership skillset to develop strategies and techniques to reach the needs of families, homes, schools and communities with the church serving as the coordinator to bring these institutions together to establish meaningful dialogue and reachable goals for all of the citizens who reside in the communities.

Parents – husbands and wives, mothers and fathers – these are the people who have come out of the various institutions of learning. They are the foundation that teach their children the basic skills of learning, how to communicate their names and addresses, how to pray, develop relationships with families, relatives, and others, personal needs, personal property and respect for people. These are some basics that a child needs in order to be ready for school, and function in each developmental stage of growth and maturity as they become involved in their families, schools, churches and communities.

The Great Commission – Matthew 28:18-20

Many family members are not connected to any congregations. They are lost because the church has lost its drawing power to convince people that the church has a powerful teaching ministry to reach the needs of the total family. Those needs of the family can be met for children, adults and parents in classes that focus on the biblical teaching of life and happiness, peace and prosperity, hell and sin, and death.

With social, moral and educational teaching, the church helps family members become well rounded in their day to day living, preparing them to become well rounded persons capable of contributing to their family, church and community. Let us not forget Jesus knew what he was teaching to his disciples and explained it to them, and conquered them. If there is no sin, we do not need a Savior. If we do not need a Savior, we do not need preachers. The churches and the preachers need to do a better job in teaching about sin and hell.

At some churches, preaching about sin and hell have become off limits. You just don't hear those fire and brimstone, going to hell sermons in your main line denominations as you once did years ago. In those cases, the more training pastors receive in seminary, the less preaching you hear about sinful living, and the more you hear about social gospel and prosperity living.

I read an article of a pastor who had a counseling session with one of his married couples, because they were not getting along. The husband blurted out, "I don't believe in hell." But after he and his wife explained their adulteries, their angers, their jealousies; and their hurts, Pastor said, "You don't have to believe in hell; you are experiencing it." Many people have formed the thought that you are living in hell on this earth when you are having problems with poverty, sickness, loneliness, hopelessness, and loss of meaning and broken relationships.

There is a process of bringing together these people to form a more perfect union in the church and community. It's a molding process, it's an instructional process, and it's a baptizing process in the name of the Father, and of the Son, and of the Holy Ghost. The closing promise, though given to the apostles, is transmitted to every generation of believers.

My prayer is not for them alone. I pray also for those who will believe in me through their message," (John 17:20)

PILLAR III: The Church

Christ's promise of His presence, "I am with you always", guarantees the success of the church's mission because it is really His mission carried out by His called-out disciples. The phrase unto the end of the world means until the end of the age. Therefore Christ's empowerment of the church to evangelize to the world is available in every age, even unto the end of the church age. In comparing the Great Commission with Jesus Christ's promise to continually build His church, we must conclude that He intended His church always to be spiritually militant and evangelistically aggressive as we take his claims of lordship to the entire world one generation at a time, but each generation participating.

> "And Jesus came and spoke unto them, saying, all power is given unto me in heaven and earth. Go ye therefore, and teach all nations, baptizing them in the name of the Father, and of the Son, and of the Holy Ghost: Teaching them to observe all things whatsoever I have commanded you: and lo, I am with you always, even unto the end of the world."
> Matthew 28:18-20

The controlling purpose of the local church is to make disciples of all people, and to teach all kinds of people on how to live an abundant life. The teaching process must be prayerful, biblical, prophetic and educational in order to reach the people who need to be discipled. It must be done by committed persons who have been trained by committed disciples who understand they are the keepers of their brothers and sisters, which are made in God's image. God wants all people to be saved – the sinners, the poor, the wealthy, gay or straight, sick and shut-ins, the lame, the mentally ill, homeless, incarcerated, abused, rejects, lonely, educators and others.

PILLAR III: The Church

In Christianity, the Great Commission is the instruction of the resurrected Jesus Christ to his disciples to spread his teachings to all the nations of the world.

The Great Commission is a command which involves three steps: Evangelism, Baptism and Education. The Church at Jerusalem saturated the communities, neighborhoods and surrounding towns with the gospel. The Lord is expecting the local churches to use the same strategies to reach the un-churched wherever they are, in your neighborhoods, on your job and in your communities. All Christians should understand their active membership in the church for Christ is an active process that keeps the church's membership growing and on fire for generations to come.

The Great Commission brings the gospel into the hearts where the people are. The Great Commission is a process of reaching where they are. Jesus is using his authority to send people out into the world. The Great Commission is not just an order, but a pronouncement of victory by the risen Savior through His disciples. All power or authority is now in the hands of Christ, in heaven and on earth. On the basis of that authority and power the Christian disciples are to carry out the Great Commission of the church. Go ye, is a force of command: "Go."

The Church is the voice that moves the people to become missionary minded. The church is the vehicle of Christ's mission that moves and finds people wherever they are. The movement never stops because people are always waiting to be saved. People are waiting to become trained disciples. People are waiting to be asked to enter into a commitment where they can be trained by a learned person who knows how to teach, how to challenge people to become involved in reaching the lives of others. There are people in every congregation who are waiting to be asked. Are you willing to

PILLAR III: The Church

commit yourselves to three hours per week of extensive training to reach people who are lost in the world for not knowing Jesus Christ as their savior?

The training helps individuals understand scriptural foundations based on the teaching of our Lord Jesus Christ, and enable each person to gain more knowledge on how to become a team leader in the local church by assuming one of the leadership roles of working members in the local church; to reach those who are lost.

The Salt of the Earth and the Light of the World

Jesus called his disciples to meet him in Galilee on a mountain top where he had chosen to continue the sermon he had attempted to preach in the Jewish Synagogues to the Jewish people. They rejected his teaching and instructed him to get out of the temple and out of their community. The messages of the Beatitudes (Matthew 5:3-12) are followed by Jesus preaching and teaching on the character of the Christian's life as salt and light.

> "Ye are the salt of the earth: but if the salt has lost his flavor, wherewith shall it be salted? It's thenceforth good for nothing, but to be cast out, and to trodden under the foot of me." Matthew 5:13

In Matthew 5:13, again the phrase "ye are" indicates that only the genuinely born-again person is salt and can help meet the needs of the world. Ye are the light of the world describes the essential mission of the Christian to the world. He is the condition (salt) to meet world's needs and he has a mission (light) to the world. His light is to clearly shine forth into the darkness of human depravity. He is to set his light upon a candlestick, not hide it under a bushel, that is, a basket. Darkness is the absence of light; and darkness alone dispels the light, but the smallest light can dispel the great darkness.

> **14** "You are the light of the world. A city that is set on a hill cannot be hidden. **15** Nor do they light a lamp and put it under a basket, but on a lampstand, and it gives light to all *who are* in the house. **16** Let your light so shine before men, that they may see your good works and glorify your Father in heaven." Matthew 5:14-16

Christ's teaching in these Beatitudes is highlighting His prophets preaching on simple words that are meaningful and powerful to his disciples as they are to go forth into their neighborhoods and world to become salt and light wherever they go. Jesus reminded them they are the salt of the earth, and the light of the world. The prophets, who went before them, were salt of the land of Canaan; but the apostles are to become salt of the whole earth. They are charged and given order by Jesus Christ to go into the world to preach the gospel.

How could they go forth into the entire world and preach the Gospel of Jesus Christ? How could they go forth into their neighborhoods and community? By walking, teaching as they came in contact with people on the streets, in the market places and on the roads; wherever they came in contact with people. But in the whole wide world, that's a different order and seems impossible for men, but "with God, all things are possible." (Matthew 19:26) They are the salt of the earth, and the light of the world. Salt preserves, it penetrates, it cleanses; it is relishing, and preserves for purification.

Salt is an everlasting covenant that is called a covenant of salt (Numbers 18:19), and the gospel is an everlasting gospel. Salt was required in all the sacrifices. Christians, and especially ministers, are the salt of the earth. Ministers, laity, leaders of various groups ought to be the salt that moves within the hearts and minds of people as they work with them in all of

PILLAR III: The Church

the services they are called to perform for the people as they relate to them in their daily responsibilities.

They are the good salt and broken into many grains, but very useful and necessary. What they are to be in themselves- seasoned with the gospel, with salt of grace! You must have salt in yourself or else you cannot diffuse it among others. What they are to be to others, they must not only be good, but they should do good. What a great blessing they are to the world! Christ sent his disciples into the entire world to teach, preach, and compel men and women, boys and girls to accept the teaching of our Lord and savior Jesus Christ.

The salt and light of the world messages are now heard in villages, neighborhoods, communities, towns, cities and metropolitans areas all over the world. This message of Jesus Christ is preached from temples, churches, mission fields, tents, street corners, conferences, conventions, radios, TV stations and you name it! This move of God started from a village mountain top in Canaan of Galilee many thousands of years ago.

When the gospel is preached with convincing power, souls are saved, lives are changed, broken relationships are restored, and repentance and forgiveness take place. The teaching and preaching of the Gospel is to be shared by all persons who believe in the Lord and Savior Jesus Christ as the salt and light of the world. They are the seasoned power because of their relationships as they work and move among the people in their daily work with the people of God.

Where there is no power, you find boarded up buildings, dying schools and neighborhoods. That resulted in lower tax collections for schools, and operations for city services. It is now time for citizens who love their community and know what is right, to come together in the spirit of the Lord to give

PILLAR III: The Church

their time and commitment to their church, school and community. This will help us to have peaceful homes, and neighborhoods where children may run and play; a place where family members will feel safe in their homes, on the streets and not worry if they will be robbed or killed in their own neighborhoods.

It is time for churches to use the power that God has given to them to teach, teach, teach, and teach until changes are seen in the lives of people who are living in fear 24 hours a day, 7 days a week. Change must occur in the communities where there is poverty, abuse, bad relationships, addictions, homelessness, joblessness, broken homes without a father or mother, and where children are neglected by their parents and relatives. It's time for families to realize if improvements don't happen in the home and church, they are not going to happen in the schools and communities.

Ways of being salt and light

The Church, more than any other organization or institution in the community, was not founded only for persons holding membership; it was founded by God's Son, Jesus Christ, to be the greatest moving institution of the world. The Church is the moving power that travels through the hearts of people in their leadership roles as parents, family members, leaders of ministries, teachers, judges, mayors and other elected officials, business owners, police officers, and all persons who are committed – wherever they may be – to stand up for the teaching of our Lord Jesus Christ.

Our churches must become the focal point where the people are to witness, to teach and to win souls to help save dying communities. Communities that are dying affect families, neighborhoods, schools and churches! How can the church do nothing, when they see what is taking place in their community?

PILLAR III: The Church

The church is the moral center that teaches the value of life, responsibilities to families, schools, and communities to become a unit working together by understanding its responsibilities! A community is at its best when families, schools and churches are working together. When a community has crime, drug wars, gang fighting, poverty, homelessness, low self-esteem, and loss of jobs, consistent dropouts, and poor schools that are not meeting the needs of the children or its people – it is a community that is dying!

Information plus motivation equals action. There are many ways you can determine if a church has an action program. If a church is in the heart of a community and most of the homes need major improvements to bring them up to city code where streets and sidewalks need repairs, street and alley lights are not working or need to be installed, that church is in violation. If children are running the streets night and day, dropouts rates are high, parents have lost control of their children and there is no respect for the church property, or private property, graffiti and gang signs are throughout the community and there is no respect for the worshippers when they come to church on Sunday or weekdays or nights activities; if your church is located in a community like this, it has violated the commission of Jesus Christ.

There are congregations telling neighbors they don't want them in your church, and neighbors telling the church they don't want them in their neighborhood. Every church that I have pastored I knew the families that resided in the neighborhood. The pastor and the membership must show a friendly attitude toward the people when they enter into their neighborhood. They must take time and speak to them and find out how they are doing and invite them to come and worship and become a part of their fellowship.

PILLAR III: The Church

Find out if they have a block club and if they don't, invite them to come to the church and organize one. Have one of your ministries to host the meeting and serve refreshments. Show the neighbors you love them and motivate them by doing special things for their children and adults by organizing tutorial classes, and charm clubs for children. You may need to have parenting classes: Home making, budgeting, family planning, health and recreation for adults and family members.

Churches and communities working together is a process that happens when leaders recognize that something needs to be done. When citizens come together to discuss and define what the problems are in their communities, that's when action takes place. When enough people see the issues and begin to talk, pray, fellowship about what they see, and when citizens mobilize themselves into an action plan, the neighborhood will become organized by working together to correct any problems or situations in their communities.

Pastors, teachers, doctors, lawyers, health care providers, CEO's, business owners and all persons who are in the professional job markets gave some serious thought about what they wanted to do for the rest of their lives. And the best way was through mentoring and testing processes. Too many of our children are graduating from college and don't know what they want to do, because of the rule you must go to college or some technical schools. The schools, churches and communities must do a better job of preparing our children for their chosen professions.

Soul Winning

While we continue to use these methods, new soul-winning and new institutes and tracts inform the people how to be soul-winners, the truth of the matter is that most of them simply do not want to be soul-winners! They have information, but not sufficient motivation. If they had to, most Christians could probably tell someone *how* to accept Christ as their personal savior, but, they just do not do it! As the most enlightened age in history, it is obvious that the reason we do so little is that information – knowing what to do, is not being coupled with motivation or the desire to do what we know.

To know what to do is human. To do what we know is divine! In my pastoral experiences as a pastor and Presiding Elder, I have noticed there were pastors who were assigned to certain congregations and stayed there for one or two years, and at the end of each year no growth in membership, and another pastor was assigned, growth took place. What's the difference? Attitude and Personality!

As a man thinks in his heart, so is he. The pastor with the right attitude thought in his heart that he could do all things through Christ who strengthens him; therefore he was able to add growth to the membership. The pastor who didn't know membership growth approaches the situation with failure in mind and that's why he or she fails in all of their pastoral appointments.

Motivation begins with enthusiasm. When pastors and congregations approach the situation with failure in mind, that's why they fail. I heard an evangelist preaching a sermon in a revival, and he told about this pastor who awoke in the middle of the night to find the church house ablaze. And, who should be leading the bucket brigade, throwing water on the fire, but the town's atheist! "Atheist," said the preacher, "I've never seen your church on fire before!"

Let the church get on fire and the world will come and watch it burn! With the exception of those congregations that are showing more growth than loss, there are too many of our congregations and denominations who have reached a level where there seems to be little growth of membership due to deaths and membership dropouts.

PILLAR III: The Church

The Pastor as the Leader

The pastor as the leader of the congregation must show leadership and administrative skills as he or she moves through the congregation. The pastor is to lead the flock. The flock is not to lead the pastor. The pastor is the Good Shepherd, he knows his members by names, where they live, where they work, he knows what schools the churches' children are attending. He knows the children by name and their relationship to family members. As the pastor you are the leader, act like the leader, and talk like the leader and for God's sake, dress like the leader.

You don't have to dress in clergy shirt collars and clergy suits. But be clean and neat at all times. Don't be afraid to lead your people. If you don't lead them somebody else will take over the leadership role. You are not a dictator; you are the pastor in charge to lead, to plan and work with your Official Board

PILLAR III: The Church

and Leadership Team under the leadership of our Lord and Savior Jesus Christ.

This is the leadership from the Father for you. The church, of course, must always give final approval. Develop a close relationship in order to establish a clear understanding of your vision for the church. As pastor, you should take hold of your leadership role. At the same time you must have the personality to work with your Official Board and Leadership Team to bring them on the same page with you. By remaining open and transparent you will earn the respect, and decision making won't be as combative.

It is imperative that you listen to each person. Let me repeat, listen to each person, and find out who they are, and where they are. A good leader will listen and observe how they express themselves and what they know in general, and the tone in which they express themselves on various subjects. It may be wise to meet with some of your team members one on one in order to get a spiritual perception of the person, and overview of the congregation's vision. Be available to meet with your leaders and membership. Be faithful, be on time for your appointments, meetings and worship services. Have office hours and be there in your office when you are supposed to be there. Many times members will be in the area and just want to stop by and say hello to their pastor.

I remember when I was pastoring where the church parsonage was on the alley right behind the church. The congregation had authorized the trustees to go forth and bring back three recommendations to the church membership for a more suitable home. The Trustees and I met, and we followed their recommendations by looking at several beautiful homes and prepared the file with the cost of the house, location and monthly payments. The trustees presented the plan to the membership and the membership voted it down. One of the trustees made a motion not to accept the plan because it didn't give the age of the house or the yearly taxes on the house. I got angry and told the people that I was not going to live in an alley house with my family. None of them were living that way; and I could not have my family living that way!

One of the trustees made a statement and said, "Pastor, the only thing the membership is asking for is the age of the house and the taxes per year and we will have that ready next Sunday." The meeting adjourned. One of mothers of the church came to me and whispered, "Don't worry pastor. We are going to get that house for our pastor and his family, don't worry, we love you all." The following Sunday the vote was taken and no one voted against it. It's imperative for the pastor and leadership team to do a thorough job in preparing their reports, finding and making sure all pertinent information is included in the presentation before bringing it to the Church conference for a vote.

You must realize that you have a cross section of leaders and members within a congregation. Several of them are very knowledgeable in a variety of subjects because of the type of work duties they perform on their jobs every day. As pastors and leaders in all walks of life, no matter what professional skills the members may hold you must think big. You must make big plans and work with them to succeed in a big way. In order for all to be successful with your plans, big or small, you must keep positive people around you. If you don't, negative people will destroy your entire plan.

Negative people are like little men who think little and expect little things to happen. Jesus said, "For as he thinketh in his heart, so is he:" Proverbs 23:7. Leaders must be positive about everything they do in life. Have you ever thought about Jesus Christ's command he gave his disciples?

PILLAR III: The Church

> And Jesus came and spake unto them, saying, All power is given unto me in heaven and in earth. Go ye therefore, and teach all nations, baptizing them in the name of the Father, and of the Son, and of the Holy Ghost: Matthew 28:18 – 19

Jesus expects big things to come from the directions He gives to His pastors, leaders and Christians. He promised He will be with them when they go on his mission journey in the communities where they live and work. Sometimes the church's leadership gets lost by thinking they are to go to Galilee, Jerusalem or some foreign land overseas. In essence Jesus is expecting us to be teachers in our homes, schools, churches and communities by compelling boys and girls, men and women to accept the teaching of our Lord and Savior Jesus Christ.

The challenge is that you must think big as you go forth on your mission to meet family members who have never been involved. Some have never been inside a church building, the closest they have ever gotten to a church is when they walked by the front of church buildings. The harvest is plenty, but the labors are few. Your relationship with God and people are the only way to survive the uncertainties that confront you each day. Among those uncertainties are the news media, local, state, national, and international influences; crime, housing, economics, education, health insurance and transportation.

God is concerned with healthy relationships. Healthy relationships come from God's Church families working on one accord to accomplish the needs of families: jobs, decent housing, health insurance, safe environment, good schools, parks and communities that are safe 24 hours a day, 7 days a week. These concerns are brought to the leadership of the church who vocalize them to community leaders who work

PILLAR III: The Church

together with their political leaders in order to affect positive outcomes in the community.

Certainly, our world and society are filled with many social ills. These ills are attacking the foundation of our society. I raise the question: Can our society continue in the direction it is headed and remain the strong fabric family God has created? I don't think so.

Unity

When God's people are united they are able to change the direction of the moral erosion that is destroying the foundation of families and neighborhoods. Our community has become so preoccupied with technologies (computers, cell phones, TV, movie productions, dress codes, and language), that we will accept anything in homes, churches and schools.

Since God's Church is the only institution in the world that has a membership of all kinds of people (the rich, the poor, blacks, whites, Jews and Gentiles, sick and healthy, LGBT, reject and well, married and divorced), these are the people with power that comes from repenting, praying, fasting, and tarring. They are the converts, they are the leaders, and they have been trained in the doctrine of the Church membership class. They are baptized with water and filled with the Holy Ghost that comes from the Lord Jesus Christ. All they need to do is to come together just as they are, with a willing spirit to do the will of God, as God has promised His people:

> "If my people, which are called by my name, shall humble themselves, and pray, and seek my face, and turn from their wicked ways; then will I hear from heaven, and will forgive their sins, and will heal their land." 2nd Chronicles 7:14 *KJSB*

PILLAR III: The Church

God promised his people that he owned a house and prepared it for all people to come; pray and He will answer their prayers. God's Prayer House is for all people who reside in the neighborhoods and are committed to enter into the house of prayer to ask God to bring healing in the land. In those days when God appeared to Solomon, the concerns were: famine, pestilence, wars, and locusts devouring the land, enemies and greed.

Today's issues in the land are: broken relationships in the family, crime, weather, war, sickness, moral erosion, dropouts, lack of quality of life, lack of jobs, employments, lack of health insurance, and inability of churches to have a greater impact in their neighborhoods where their churches are located. And there seems to be more crimes in the neighborhoods where Black churches are located than any other neighborhood. I believed God is telling us as He told Solomon in his day; it is time for churches to get their act together.

Take a stroll or ride through the Black neighborhoods. What do you see? Churches burned out, houses and buildings that are defaced with graffiti, denoting gang territories, prostitution, drugs and crack houses, and overall run-down neighborhoods. From what we see I believed that God is calling on Black churches, their pastors, leadership and membership to come together just as he called Solomon in Biblical days. God promised three majors points:
1. God promised to own this house for a house of sacrifice to Israel and a house of prayer for all people. He promised His name shall be there forever.
2. He promised to answer the prayers of his people that should be made. National judgments are here, supposed famine and pestilence, and perhaps war, for by the locusts devouring the land, may be meant enemies as greedy as locust, and laying all waste. National

PILLAR III: The Church

repentance, prayer, and reformation, are required. National mercy is then promised, that God will forgive their sin, which brought the judgment upon them, and then healed their land, redress all their grievances. Pardoning mercy makes way for healing mercy.
3. He promised to perpetuate Solomon's kingdom upon conditions that he preserve in his duty. But he set before him death as well as life, the curse as well as the blessing. He supposed it possible that though they had this temple built to the honor of God, yet they might be drawn aside to worship other gods. He threatened it as certain that, if they did so, it would certainly be the ruin of both church and state.

Commentary on The Whole Bible by Matthew Henry 2 Chronicles 7:12-22 page 4

God is calling for national judgments, national repentance for all churches, neighborhoods and communities to come together and pray for changes to be made. God is expecting the church to take the leadership role in making positive changes that need to be made if we are going to save our neighborhoods and communities.

PILLAR III: The Church

Unity

I dreamed I stood in a studio
And watched two sculptors there,
The clay they used was a young child's mind
And they finished it with care.

One was a teacher; the tools he used
Were books and music and art;
One a parent with a guiding hand
And a gentle and loving heart.

Day after the teacher toiled
With a touch that was deft and sure
While the parent labored by his side
And polished and smoothed it o'er.

And when at last their task was done
They were proud of what they had wrought,
For the things they has molded into the child
Could neither be sold nor bought

And each agreed he would have failed
If he had worked alone.

For behind the parent stood the school
And behind the teacher, the home.

Anonymous 1998

From the One Church One School Parenting Workshop
Dr. Cordia P. Moore, Assistant to the Superintendent – Gary School District

National Judgment

In 1 Kings 5:13-14, King Solomon *(LAB, NIV)* conscripted laborers from all of Israel – thirty thousand men. He sent them off to Lebanon in shifts of ten thousand a month, so that they spent one month in Lebanon and two months at home. Adoniram was in charge of the force labor.

When Solomon was building the Temple, he knew that God wanted him to have enough workers per schedule and not to interfere with family life activities. God knew that family life

PILLAR III: The Church

was imperative for the Temple growth and did not want family members to be absent from the home for an extended time from the family. He knew that a father's absence from the home would place a determinant effect upon the children's lives and the wife.

A father was not only the supporter of his family; he was the enforcer of the rules of the family. He taught the word of God to his family, he instructed his children to be respectful to each other, and the role the family members were to play in building a strong community and become active in the community affairs. The concern of Solomon for the people played a major role in the family while the fathers and men of the homes and community were about making a living and providing for their family members. He showed his concern for the welfare of his workers and the importance he placed on building family life.
The strength of a nation is in direct proportion to the strength of its families. Solomon wisely recognized that family should always be a top priority. As you structure your own work or arrange the schedules of others, take care to consider how your plans impact your families.

Over the last sixty years, I have watched the break down in family structure in their participations in churches activities. For example, I have observed families coming to Sunday school and worship services together. Then I began noticing the fathers and other men absent from Sunday school and Worship services. I raised the question to family members regarding their fathers and men of the church, and I was informed that their schedules had changed and they had to work on Sundays.

I later learned that some of the men had to work every Sunday. That was the way their schedules were written. Because of the job market in the area and the demand of steel

PILLAR III: The Church

from the steel mills, automobile plants, truck drivers, factory workers, and other related jobs, it interfered with men attending Sunday worship services. I often think about those days when fathers and others had to work on Sundays, and the church failed to meet their spiritual needs by not providing a structural worship service to reach the spiritual needs on days they were not working. The better plan would have offered worship opportunities such as Wednesday or Saturday evenings or afternoons.

My First Pastorate

My first pastorate was in St. Joseph, MO. I came out of the great St. John C.M.E. Church in Detroit, Michigan, where Rev W.A. Amos was the pastor, and was later elected Bishop in our great Zion the C.M.E. Church. I took note of his successes and failures. I made a promise when I got a church I would hold worship services for one hour; 11:00 am to 12:00 noon. On my first Sunday the service started at 11:00 am and closed at 12:00 noon. The next Sunday, one of the members spoke to me as she was leaving the sanctuary and said: "Pastor, Haste Makes Waste!" The next Sunday this lady said the same thing after leaving the service, "Pastor, Haste, Makes waste!" The Lord told me to give this lady a call, so I called her on Monday morning, and asked her how she was doing, and she told me she was doing fine.

She said "Pastor let me tell you something young man!"
I said, "Yes ma'am."
"You stop preaching those 15 minute popcorn sermons, with the congregation singing two verses of those powerful hymns of the church, and the choir only singing two verses of their selections. Don't you know what your members are doing when they leave church on Sunday morning?"
I said "No ma'am."

PILLAR III: The Church

"They are stopping at the Baptist, Methodist and Church of God In Christ churches, that's what they are doing, and the next thing some of them will be joining those congregations!" I said, "Thank you sister."

On Thursday night I met with the choir members and discussed with them the worship service format. I noticed some of them began to smile and said, "That's fine pastor we have always done it that way." It is imperative for pastors, leaders, and the membership to have a good working relationship. Know your members; because your members want to help you succeed. Watch how you respond to them. Don't cut them off because you may be upset, or have a personal agenda toward them because of their age or gender, personality or the way they look or talk. These are your people and they are willing to stand with you, pray for you and your family.

These saints loved their church, they have been there before you were born, and many of the members have invested their resources and money by paying utility bills, conference claims, buying paint, church outdoor signs and beautifying the lawn around the church, and sacrificed in order for the church to reach its status in the community. Be careful how you move through the membership and through the community because they are watching every move you make!

God Will Make a Way

My wife prepared a grocery list for me one Saturday morning to go to the grocery store, and I didn't have enough money to buy all the items that were on the list. I walked out of the back door to go to the grocery store, and on my way to the store I walked behind the city auditorium where there were activities every Friday night, and there was an envelope in the alley with $30.00, no name on it. All I could to say was "Thank you Jesus, the Lord will make a way somehow." Remember, don't try to force something; watch God work on your behalf.

My First Wedding

I got a call one Friday morning from a neighbor, who asked me if I would come to her house to perform a wedding. My answer was, "Yes." I had heard that this house had some special activities going on at that location. I picked up my ritual book and went to the house and met the couple. This was my first couple to perform a wedding, and my first interracial wedding. We had a very friendly discussion and they explained to me who they were, that they were in love, and they wanted to get married. I performed the ceremony and prayed the prayer of blessing upon them for many years to come.

The gentleman gave me $25.00 for the service. I return to my office and prayed and asked the Lord to forgive me if I had done anything wrong. I made a promise to God that I would never perform another wedding without premarital counseling. That commitment has been kept as of that day, from 1960 to 2014, and I have performed and participated in more than 150 weddings. (Premarital Counseling information will be included in the appendix of this book.)

One Saturday I was leaving the parsonage to perform a wedding for two of the young adults of the church, our daughter saw me walking down the sidewalk, and she asked her mother where I was going. My wife told her that I was going to perform a marriage ceremony for Sugar and Joe. She asked her mother if I was going to marry Sugar, what they were going to do. My wife explained to her that I was going to perform a wedding for two persons in order for them to become husband and wife. She was then able to understand how families are developed through marriage.

PILLAR III: The Church

Marriage
Marriage is a sacred Institution ordained and Regulated by God's Word. It is a divine institution between a man and a woman.

Marriage is not easy. It is not a rose garden. Although there are times when it can be rosy, God did say that we will have trials and tribulations. Jesus said, "All things are possible; with him."

Prayer
Prayer is necessary to unite couples and to remain united. Prayer is necessary in everything we do. Counseling was extremely important prior to marriage.

Reflections on Marriage by Cathy Clarett

Pre-marital counseling was no part of the process when I got married, but I believe the benefits are many. It is highly unlikely that a couple would have this type of conversation by themselves. These thoughts are mine after 40 years of marriage, and having attended a marriage ministry workshop at the Israel CME Church and talking to others who have had this type of counseling.

Personality traits are often uncovered in these discussions that can help you understand your mate's "personality type." This can avoid conflicts in the future because when he or she has a certain reaction to a situation, you shouldn't take it personally. Just know that it is a result of their personality type. This can also help you know the best way to confront them or tackle a problem when it occurs.

When you marry someone, you are getting more than one person. They are your primary loyalty but you inherit other family members and relationships. Be respectful of these and do not interfere or try to change them. Be yourself and try to establish your own relationship and closeness with these individuals if they allow it but don't push it.

Both partners should feel free to express their thoughts and opinions in the marriage and perform the functions they do best – these are not set in stone. Sometimes the husband may be the better cook or have more patience in dealing with children. These responsibilities must be shared but don't expect it to be 50/50. Just try to make it add up to 100.

It is important to most men to feel they are the head of the marriage and he should be. Not in the sense of a boss or dictator but as an example and spokesman for decisions you have come to agreement on after joint discussions. A man can only be an effective head when his instructions come from GOD. When he bases his actions on the teachings of GOD, it should not be a problem for the wife to be "obedient." The order must be GOD-Husband-Wife.

Communication is essential for growth. But what is communication? We most often think of talking. But words are possibly the least honest and least effective means to communicate. It's easy to say something and words are open to interpretation. You should observe each other honestly— pay attention. Learn what your spouse is saying through facial expressions, body language and actions. After all, "seeing is believing." Communicate as you would with a pet or child. When they cry out, it is a plea for some type of help. Honest observation of your spouse can help you recognize needs they cannot verbalize.

You must be equally yoked. The biblical expression speaks of 2 oxen pulling a cart together. One cannot outpace the other. They have to fall into a rhythm with each other-pulling as a team or the cart will topple over. It is the same with a

PILLAR III: The Church

marriage. Both partners must be equally invested in the relationship and willing to do what it takes to make it work. This involves a lot of emotional comprise. One spouse may have to back off and the other slow down to establish this rhythm so they can be "as one." This can apply to all situations within the marriage. It is similar to 2 rugby players running down the field together passing the ball between them. It's not about moving fast – the main goal is to support each other, depend on each other to be there to catch the ball so they can move forward together.

It is important to know that being "as one" does not mean that each person is not an individual. You need to be a whole person before you marry someone. Your wholeness comes from your relationship with yourself and GOD. When you are not whole, you may depend on your spouse to complete you and to fulfill all of your needs. This is not possible! This unrealistic expectation often leads to disappointment with the marriage and with your spouse. Marriage does not follow the mathematical rule that $\frac{1}{2} + \frac{1}{2} = 1$. In this case, $1 + 1 = $ One.

You must love each other. I don't know what makes one person love another, but when you don't know what to do, pray; do nothing and remember that GOD says, "Love never fails."

Testimonials

Reverend Cargle counseled George and me. It has been extremely helpful. There are important issues that you need to discuss prior to marriage.

Here are some of the issues that need to be discussed.

1. Finances
2. Debt
3. Family Members/Extended Family
4. Children
5. Likes and Dislikes

PILLAR III: The Church

6. Church
7. Respect
8. Conflict

Love is the nucleus in marriage. Take time and discuss issues and problems with your spouse. Be a good listener. Learn to disagree with one another in a loving and civil manner.

Marriage is not always 50%/50%. There are times when it is 90/10, 80/20 or 70/30.

Be compassionate with one another. Don't be abusive to each other. Treat one another with respect. There are times when you must have common sense. Be careful in regard to outside information about your spouse, you must put forth an effort to work together. A divided house cannot stand. Every comment does not warrant a reply. There are times that you just need to listen. Help is needed in the home. Do not expect one to do everything. Exercise is good for all of us. Assist and work together in keeping the house tidy. You can remain a couple with God, Prayer and Love. Jesus said, "In all thy ways acknowledge me and I will direct your path."

George and Earnestine Williams

Elder Carrell K. Cargle gave marriage counseling to George and Earnestine Williams prior to our marriage August 24, 1974. This was important and helpful. Marriage is always a work in progress.

We were married on July 5, 1969 at Israel CME Church in Gary, IN by Rev. Carrell K. Cargle, Sr. After almost 46 years of marriage, we have found that money management (which was included in Rev. Cargle's pre-marital counseling) has been a not so obvious factor that can have a negative effect on a marriage.

As newlyweds, we both brought different attitudes about money management to our marriage based on our life experiences up until that point. Our attitudes were different, but not quite at opposite ends of the spectrum, but regardless, we quickly learned that they needed to be aligned in order to make our marriage a success. We both had the same vision for our life together and for our family. We both had extremely strong work ethics; therefore it was a matter of agreeing on how to achieve that vision. We had to find the right balance of creating financial stability (current and long term) through budgeting

PILLAR III: The Church

while still leaving just enough to have a little fun. Well into our marriage, as our faith in God increased, we made the decision to become tithers, which has definitely been a blessing. As Luke 6:38 states, "Give and it will be given back to you. Good measure, pressed down, shaken over, will be put into your lap. For with the measure you use it will be measured back to you."

With prayer and by setting a good example, we have been blessed to have raised two beautiful daughters and instilled in them a strong work ethic and a responsible attitude towards money management in their marriages.

We thank God for the blessings that we've received in our marriage and we thank Rev. Cargle for planting the seed.

James and Rita McGee

Home Visitation

One of the stewards informed me one of the members of the church was hospitalized. He told me which hospital she was in and also brought me up to date on who she was and her occupation of running a special event house. He dropped the word and told me pastor I don't think you should go there to her home. I told this good steward, God had called me to pastor the sick and well, and I reminded him what Jesus said in his relationship with his Disciples:

> "For I was hungry, and ye gave me meat: I was thirsty and ye gave me drink: I was a stranger, and ye took me in Naked and ye clothed me: I was sick, and ye visited me: I was in prison, and ye came to see me. Then shall the righteous answer him, saying, Lord, when saw ye thee a hungered, and fed thee? Or thirsty, and gave thee drink? When saw we thee a stranger, and took thee in? Or naked, and clothed thee? Or when sow we thee sick, or in prison, and you came unto thee? And the King shall answer and say unto them, Verily I say unto you, Inasmuch as ye have done it unto one of the least of these my brethren, ye have done it unto me."
> Matthew 25: 35-40.

PILLAR III: The Church

Visiting the sick, healing broken hearts and restoring broken relationships is one of the great callings of a pastor. The next day I stopped by to see her and I noticed there were several young ladies looking out of the window.

I stepped to the door and pressed the door bell, the young ladies vanished and the member came to the door and invited me in, and I had a wonderful visit with her. She brought me up to date on so many things, and she was so delighted that I stopped by to see her. I prayed with her to have a blessed and healthy relationship with the Lord and Savior Jesus Christ. I noticed that her attendance and offering improved after my visitation.

In my observation as a pastor, Presiding Elder this is one of the areas in which many congregations have neglected to fulfill its mission of church by having a spiritually-led commission on evangelism to go after those who are absent, sick, shut in, hospitalized, in nursing homes and those who are old and forgotten by the church family and family members.

Many of the old timers who supported the church and their children grew up in the church, graduated from school, college or left town to find employment are those parents who got older and gradually faded out of the membership, and the next thing you knew they are in nursing home.

Family members fail to inform the church and no follow up is done by the congregation. The new pastor has no information or a sound system to inform him or her of members they have lost sight of. Their children now are out of town and have lost contact with the church. Their mother and father loved and supported their church until they were unable to attend.

PILLAR III: The Church

Some families have formed the opinion they don't need the church anymore, so they only go on Mother's Day, Easter and Christmas. As a result, many Black families and their children are trying to live without God and moral standards. Many young people believe that all of their problems come from the outside of their community, when in fact their greatest problems come from within their own community.

There is a growing movement among young people: it is cool to have a baby, it's cool to have premarital sex; no harm can be done, it's risk free. How silly young people can become in this age to believe that. There was a folklore that once said to drink coke before having sex if you don't want to get pregnant. We all know that was incorrect. It is my prayer that the guidance teaching of the Black church will renew its efforts to regain the hold the church once had upon the Black community. The Black church must re-evangelize its community if this generation is going to be saved and become productive parents for their own children to become the leaders that God is expecting to save the world.

> "Then Pharaoh summoned Moses and Aaron. "This time I have sinned," he said to them. "The Lord is in the right, and I and my people are in the wrong. Pray to the Lord, for we have had enough thunder and hail. I will let you go; you don't have to stay any longer." Moses replied, "When I have gone out of the city, I will spread out my hands in prayer to the Lord. The thunder will stop and there will be no more hail, so you may know that the earth is the Lord's. 30 But I know that you and your officials still do not fear the Lord God." (The flax and barley were destroyed, since the barley had headed and the flax was in bloom. The wheat and spelt, however, were not destroyed, because they ripen later.) Then Moses left Pharaoh and went out of the city. He spread out his hands toward the Lord; the thunder and hail stopped, and the rain no longer poured down on the land. When Pharaoh saw that the rain and hail and thunder had stopped, he sinned again: He and his officials hardened their hearts."
> Exodus 9:27-34

PILLAR III: The Church

National Repentance

So Pharaoh's heart was hardened and he would not let the Israelites go, just as the Lord had said through Moses. It comes a time in all of our lives we must let go and face the truth that is before us. When we know we have done wrong, in sight of our brothers and sisters, and before God the Almighty. As a leader or citizen we must stand and repent to those we have lied to, mislead and knowingly we are lying, hurting our brothers and sisters just to make a point and remain popular before the people.

God is not pleased with such individuals who are in leadership positions that are misleading families, school administrators, congregations, organizations, business owners, and elected officials on local, national and international levels. In the highest level of leadership, the public accepted their leadership role and placed them on the highest spectrum of honor as a leader. Don't let your people down by falling into crooked deals, money kickbacks or shady deals. God and the people are expecting you to keep your standards above reproach at all times. If you make a mistake tell the people you were wrong, and ask them to forgive you. Don't make the same mistakes over and over or you will become a person the people will not trust.

Bonded Relationships

Since slavery, many Black families were affiliated with a church, not only were they affiliated; they were members of a church in their community. They attended Sunday school as a family, stayed for worship services as a family, and attended children and youth programs Sunday evening as a family. Mothers and fathers attended bible classes, served on usher boards, attended choir rehearsal during the week, and prayer meetings on Wednesday nights. Their faithfulness to their church and God enabled them to become a close knitted family. They reared their children in the structure of the Bible

PILLAR III: The Church

and kept them actively involved in character building programs. As the family grew and demands upon mother and father's life styles began to change in the job market, and the parents became more involved in the social world and less active in the church. This began to create problems for the whole family.

Children became less active in the church and more involved in community activities that were less concerned about the development of moral character. It has been the strength of the Black churches that have kept the community together for many years. No other agency can do the work of the church; this work is the care of the soul.

PILLAR III: The Church

Hosea, son of Beeri, was an 8th-century B.C. prophet in Israel who authored the book of prophecies bearing his name. Just as Hosea levied his charges against the religious leaders who were teaching a divided Kingdom between Jeroboam who rebelled against Solomon's son Rehoboam, and set up a rival Kingdom in the north, he also set up his own religious system (See 1 Kings 12:25-33.)

In violation of God's laws, he made two golden calves and told the people to worship them.

He also appointed his own priests, who were not descendants of Aaron. At first the residents of the Northern Kingdom continued to worship God, even though they were doing it in the wrong way, but very soon they also began to worship Canaanite gods.

Before long they had substituted Baal as their god and no longer worshipped the God of their fathers. It is not surprising that Jeroboam's false priest were unable to preserve the true worship of God.

God accused the religious leaders of keeping the people from knowing him (destroying from lack of knowledge). They were supposed to be spiritual leaders, but they had become leaders in wrong doing. The people may say to one another, if the pastor does it, it must be ok. If the teacher does it, it must be ok. If the counselor does it, it must be ok. If the movie star does it, it must be ok. If the priest does it, it must be ok. Sound familiar?

Spiritual leaderships have heavy responsibilities, whether you teach a church school class, children or youth classes, hold a church office, or lead a Bible Study, don't take your leadership responsibilities lightly. Be a leader who leads others to God.

PILLAR III: The Church

Hosea stated that the issues before the people who were sinful in their actions in Israel and in their disobedience to God. The leaders were unwilling to accept the teachings of God, and because they did not wish to be responsible for correct living, they refused to teach those under their care the true commands of God.

Who are those persons in leadership roles? They are the parents, pastors, teachers, counselors, judges and others who have been certified to teach and minister to the needs of God's people.

These leaders, through expressing and teaching the works of God to His people through workshops, seminars and one to one relationships empower people as they motivate people to better their physical, educational, moral, financial conditions. I strongly believe there are some practical ways that the churches and communities can come to a place of togetherness in resolving many of the core issues that are destroying the foundations that the communities were built on.

Parents build the foundation before the child is born and when the child arrives, they continue the process of teaching Biblical principles, how to pray their first prayer, *"Now, Lord lay me down to sleep, I pray the Lord my soul will keep, if I should die before I wake I pray the Lord my soul will keep, Lord bless mommy, dad and everybody. Amen."* This was a universal prayer that was learned by children before they could make a complete sentence. Manners, characters, respect of people, property, responsibilities and family values were also taught.

One of the major problems in the Black Communities since the early fifties is that Black Americans have struggled with the problem of broken relationships. A home without a father, single parent families, out of wedlock births, drug abuse,

PILLAR III: The Church

abused mothers living in frustration because the father of the child or children cannot be located. Too many of the mothers and fathers of children are from broken relationships.

Because of their frustration, their feeling of lack seems to take hold on their children who perhaps do not see a father image in the home and the mother is so frustrated she does not show any love toward her children. What happens when no love is shown in the home? The child or children will exit and find love in gangs, or on the streets in places where there is an attachment or a relationship is formed. It has been stated in several findings by sociologists that the major problems in the Black community today is that more than 60 to 70 percent of all babies born in the Black community were born out of wedlock. What does this have to do with it?

The answer is simple, raising a family without a father image or his influence in the home, has contributed to the breakdown of family relationships. As a result there is no voice that speaks with authority, enforces rule and regulations, and this has contributed to the rising rate of crime in the Black community.

However, I know of many cases where a single mother has done a superb job in raising her family. For instance, a single mother with a strong constitution and determination that her child is not going to get caught in gang activities shows purpose. Many single mothers keep their children involved in structural and supervised activities that include going to the library daily, reading books that are motivating to the child, and keeping a ledger of what they read. These programs enrich the children's lives, and they will become so impressed and love what they are doing. It has been proven when children are involved in character building programs their minds become adjusted and programmed to what they are involved with. Well rounded programs will not allow them to get involved in negative activities.

It has also been proven that parents, who become involved in the school's activities, help strengthen a partnership through relationship with school staff. By becoming involved with school staff, that school will become more productive compared to schools where parents are not participating.

Broken Relationships
As a father, pastor, Presiding Elder and activist in all of the cities and communities where I have lived, my experiences in working with people has enabled me to see the many problems that are causing major crisis in the Black Family. The crime in the Black community is the worst I have ever seen. We are targeting ourselves and making each other victims within our own communities. I'm talking about the type of crime that is produced by teenagers, blue collar, white collars, or activities organized by groups, gangs, pimps, or the thugs who watch their neighborhoods while family members leave their home to go to work or seek employment; returning to discover someone has broken into their homes and taken valuable jewelry, computers, TV's and anything else that is of value.

Crime is one of the major threats in the Black community. People are compelled to install alarm systems which are monitored by a security company that installed the systems, and are tied to the police department. Security doors and window systems protect what you have worked so hard to accumulate. It's those things that make your house a home and within minutes someone can break through and steal your dreams.

PILLAR III: The Church

One Church One School

The Black Families, Schools and Churches

Black families, schools and churches of all denominations have the responsibility of working together in order to save the Black community. In my opinion, Black churches have not used their hidden resources of prophetic preaching, teaching, spiritual gifts, professional expertise in finance, counseling and resources for all people in their local community; not just for those who are members of the local congregations.

Come take a journey with me; you will discover that in many churches there is not too much going on except regular programming by way of Sunday worship service, Wednesday night Bible Study/prayer service, Thursday night choir rehearsals, and Saturday children and youth activities. The ministries of the church should be designed to reach all of the people's needs, church *and* non-church members.

Church ministries should include programming which speak to the needs of parents, their family members, and senior citizens. Such programming should speak to health care, tutorial programs for children and adults, budgeting and financial planning, food pantries; all persons who have educational, spiritual, mental, moral and physical needs. These ministries need to be offered throughout the week, during hours within a day which meet the demands of the people's schedules.

The Black church is able to offer positive insights, and have influence on the lives of people who live within or outside the community where church is located. The church ought to be the standard bearer and foundation that sets guidelines and proclaims right standing by the authority which comes from the power of praying and fasting.

With the saints of God that rise early in the morning before day break asking God in the name of Jesus Christ for faithful pastors, teachers, counselors, coaches, ministers, business owners, doctors, lawyers, young and old saints of God. Saints who would become committed to the teachings of our Lord Jesus Christ, who are not ashamed to stand in the Gap on faith knowing and believing you are not alone. It is God who gives the power of holiness to stand in the Gap and transmit the Power of Jesus to the communities that are in need. The churches responsibilities are to lead all people, young and old, to a more spiritually, socially, intellectually, academically, successfully and materially prosperous lives.

PILLAR III: The Church

Those Who Stood in the Gap

In 1978 delegations of pastors, ministers and laity under the leadership of the College of Bishops and the General Secretary of Evangelism Rev. Dr. Nathanial L. Lindsey, of the Christian Methodist Episcopal Church, were called to a connectional Congress on Evangelism; to pray, study and to be empowered by the Holy Ghost to move through the C.M.E. Churches and communities where all churches were located, and to organize an early morning Power Pool.

The College of Bishops, Presiding Elders, pastors, ministers, and laity across the United States were fired up by the General Secretary's address when he challenged the attendees to go back to their communities and organize an Interdenominational Power Pool in their communities that consisted of a cross section of all faith believers from all denominations, all professions, senior citizens, young adults and family members to meet at 6:00 A.M. on Tuesday in churches, homes or community centers that would serve the needs of the people.

PILLAR III: The Church

At the time I was the pastor of Israel C.M.E. Church, and I accepted the challenge and met with the Israel delegation that was there. We prayed and sang hymns of praises and all of the members of Israel delegation accepted the challenges and committed themselves to give their support to the Power Pool by inviting members from Israel C.M.E. Church, and from the Faith community of Gary and Northwest Indiana.

We give God the praise for the founding saints of the Interfaith Power Pool who stood in the gap; Sister Myrtice Ewing, Sister Marie Gilmore, Sister Camilla Cullins, and Sister Leona Ewing of Israel C.M.E. Church, three members from Trinity Baptist Church, Sister Willie Tillman, Sister Marie Jones, and Sister Angela Jones and one from First A.M.E. Church, Sister Jean Preston. Sister Leona Ewing was Israel's Director of Evangelism, and was elected the first chairperson of The Interfaith Power Pool. The membership began to grow rapidly: within two years the attendance was too large for some homes and churches begun to welcome the Power Pool. Miracles began to happen in the Power Pool. There were many physical healing's, broken homes were restored, job opportunities became available, and unbelievers became strong kingdom builders.

PILLAR III: The Church

Spiritual Leadership Workshop

Prepared by Elder Carrell K. Cargle, Sr.

The Spiritual Leadership workshop is designed to help all leaders and members of the church become better leaders in the Body of Christ. It is my prayer that all persons will be blessed in this learning workshop and be able to translate the information learned into their own ministries.

The major key to success in any situation is the leader. This is true in business and certainly it is true in the church. In the church it is spiritual leadership that makes things happen. All Christians are called to develop their God-given talents to make the most of the lives, to develop to the fullest their God-given powers and capacities.

Jesus taught, "Whoever wants to become great among you must be your servant, and whoever wants to be first must be slave of all." (Mark 10:43-44.)

True greatness, true leadership is found in giving yourself in service to others. True service is never without cost. Often it comes with a painful situation of suffering. But the true spiritual leader is focused on the service he or she can render to God and other people, not on the residuals and perks of high office or holy titles. We must aim to put more into life than we take out.

> "The Lord has sought out a man after His own heart and appointed him leader of His people." I Samuel 13:14

PILLAR III: The Church

Calvary CME Church in Chicago
(The Little White House Church)

From Survival to Revival and Renewal of the Church by Bishop D.I. Isom, Jr. and **Focusing on the M & M's: Ministries and Members by Bishop Paul A. G. Stewart** were transformational programs presented in training sessions conducted at *The Little White House Church.*

Through Summit 2000, we were able to train exhorters, local preachers, and those on trial to understand the call to preach, the mission of the church, Book of Discipline of the C.M.E. Church and pastoral care. These training sessions were held on the second Saturdays at Calvary CME Church located at 1356 West 110th Street in Chicago where the spiritual and praying mother, Rev. Willie Tyus, pastor in charge. With her leadership team, Minister Charlotte Woods and Rev. Spencer Jones, the little White House Church was always ready for spiritual foods as well as food for the nourishment of the body. These committed servants in training learned how to become better helpers/servants in their local congregations meet the needs of God's people.

> "Go up and down the streets of Jerusalem, look around and consider, search through her squares. If you can find but one person who deals honestly and seeks the truth, I will forgive this city." Jeremiah 5:1

1. **<u>Are you a Spiritual Leader?</u>**
   Throughout the Bible, God searches for leaders.

> "I look for a man among you who would build up the wall." Ezekiel 22:30

   The Bible shows us that when God does find a person who is ready to lead, to commit to full discipleship and take on the responsibility for others, that person is used to the limit. Such leaders still have shortcomings and flaws, but despite them, they become spiritual leaders. Such were Moses, Gideon and David and those in the history of the church.

2. **<u>Do you want to be a Leader?</u>**
   To be a leader in the church one has always been required to have strength and faith beyond the mere human aspect.

   The church is painfully in need of leaders. If the world is to hear the church's voice today, leaders are needed who are authoritative, spiritual and sacrificial. Authoritative, because people desire leaders who know where they are going and confident of getting there. Spiritual, because without a strong relationship with God, even the most attractive and competent person cannot lead people to God. Sacrificial, because this follows the model of Jesus who gave himself for the whole world and who calls us to follow in His steps. Churches grow in every way when they are

PILLAR III: The Church

guided by strong spiritual leaders. The Church sinks into confusion and sickness without such leadership.

3. **Send Thou Men**

"Send thou men, that they may search the land of Canaan, which I give unto the children of Israel; of every tribe of their fathers shall ye send a man, everyone a ruler among them." Numbers 13:2

Jesus Chooses the Twelve

"And when he had called unto him his twelve disciples, he gave them power against unclean spirits, to cast them out and to heal all manner of sicknesses and all manner of disease." Matthew 10:1-4

Now the names of the twelve apostles are these: the first, Simon, who is called Peter, and Andrew his brother; James, the son of Zebedee, and John his brother; Phillip, Bartholomew, Thomas and Matthew the publican; James, the son of Alphaeus, and Lebbaeus, whose surname was Thaddeus. It was Simon the Canaanite, and Judas Iscariot, who betrayed him.

When Jesus selected his disciples, he ignored every popular idea of his day (and ours) about what kind of person could fit in the role. Jesus' band of disciples were trained and without influence. Jesus chose those men from the ranks of workers; they were not what we call professional workers who knew what Jesus wanted of them, but they were trainable. Jesus saw in them a remarkable flair. He saw in them something no one else did, and und his skillful hand they emerged as leaders who would shock the world in their devotion and commitment to Jesus.

4. **Natural Leadership Qualities**
   Too often these skills lie dormant and undiscovered. If we look carefully, we should be able to detect leadership potential in ourselves and other.

   Here are some ways to investigate your potential:
   - Have you ever broken a bad habit:
     To lead others, you must master your appetites.
   - Do you keep self-control when things go wrong?
     A leader who loses control under adversity will forfeit respect and influence.
     A leader must be calm in crisis and resilient in disappointments.
   - Do you think independently?
     A leader must use the best ideas of others to make decisions. A leader cannot wait for others to make up his or her mind.
   - Can you handle criticism: Can you profit from it?
     The humble person can learn from petty criticism; from even malicious criticism.
   - Can you turn disappointment into creative new opportunities?
   - Can you exert discipline without making it a power play?
     True leadership is an internal quality of the Spirit and needs no show of external force.
   - Are you a peacemaker?
     A leader must be able to reconcile with opponents and make peace where arguments have created hostility.
   - Are you tactful?
     Can you anticipate how your words will affect a person?
   - Can you forgive? Or do you nurse resentment and harbor ill feelings toward those who injured you?

PILLAR III: The Church

5. **Can you stand the Test?**
   These tests mean little unless we act to correct our deficits and fill the gaps of our training. Why take some of the points of weaknesses and failures you are aware of in cooperation with the Holy Spirit, who is the Spirit of discipline? Concentrate on strengthening and correcting those areas of weaknesses and faults.

   Adding leadership potentials to our lives usually requires that we shake off negative elements that hold us back. If we are overly sensitive when criticized and rush to defend ourselves, that must go. If we make excuses for failure and try to blame others or circumstances, that must go!

   If we are intolerant or inflexible so that creative people around feel hemmed in, that must go!

   If we are disturbed by anything short of perfection in ourselves and others, that must go! The perfectionist sets goals beyond his or her reach, and then sinks into guilt and falls short.

   If you cannot keep a secret, do not try to lead!

   If you cannot yield to a point when someone else's ideas are better, save yourself the frustration of failed leadership! If you want to maintain an image of infallibility, find something else to do besides leading people!

6. **The Art of Delegation**

> "And Moses chose able men out of all of Israel, and made them heads over the people, rulers of thousands, rulers of hundreds, rulers of fifties, and rulers of tens." Exodus 18:25-26

PILLAR III: The Church

And they judged the people at all seasons: the hard causes they brought unto Moses, but every small matter they judged themselves under the guidance of God.

One thing about leadership is the being able to recognize the special abilities and limitations of others; combined with capacity to help each person work in their particular God-given area. To succeed in getting things done through others is the highest type of leadership.

As a leader how do you select people to help you in your leadership role? Delegating to others the responsibilities and authority of a task is not always easy but it is necessary for the success of everyone involved. The degree to which a leader is able to delegate work is a measure of his or her success. A one-person's office can never grow larger than the load one person can carry, and sooner or later the person trying to carry all the weight will crumble under it.

7. **Jethro's Consent**
Jethro encouraged Moses by articulating a spiritual principle. "If you do this as God so commands, you will be able to stand the strain." Exodus 18:25. Jethro placed his advice under the authority of God. God takes all responsibility for enabling his servants to do their work.

If you are a president, director, teacher, superintendent, chairperson, or any other type of leader you must be ready to delegate responsibility. You as a leader must be able and willing to support your members by leading them and enabling them to become spiritual members.

8. **Findings**
When all the facts are in, swift and clear decisions are the mark of spiritual leaders. Visionaries may see, but a leader must decide. An impulsive person may be quick to declare a preference, but a leader must weigh evidence and make his or her decision on sound premises. As a spiritual leader, make sure you are operating in the will of God. As a spiritual leader you will spring into action, without regard to consequences.

Pursuing the goal, the leader never looks back or calculates escape strategies if plans turn sour. Nor do true leaders cast blame for failure on subordinates.

The spiritual leader will not procrastinate when faced by a decision, nor vacillate after making it. To postpone decisions is really to decide for the status quo. In most decisions the key element is not so much knowing what to do, but in living with the results.

References
- The King James Study Bible
- Spiritual Leadership by J Oswald Sanders
- 20/20 Vision by Dale E Galloway
- How to Have a Better Relationship with Anybody by James Hilt
- 2002 CME Discipline
- Serving From the Heart by Resurrection Resources, Abingdon Press

PILLAR III: The Church

Ministry Beyond the Walls

All local congregations must ask one fundamental question. Does God call, command and expect the church to be large in numbers? While many will answer this question negatively, all would agree that it would be expected all congregation souls be growing.

Two factors enter into our understanding of all congregations growing. God commands us to love God with all our heart, soul, mind and strength and to love neighbor as ourselves *(Luke 10:25-28.)* God gives us the commission in *Matthew 28:18-20* to make disciples of all. This love and the commission give emphasis To God's concern for inclusion of all people.

Congregations are surrounded with people who are not included inside the walls of the church. Many of those who are in our communities are excluded. Some of the exclusion has to do with the church finding it hard and overwhelming to minister to the community in which it finds itself. Many communities have changed over the years, yet many times the church is not equipped for the change that has taken place. Often we even perceive of those outside the church walls, our new neighbors, as enemies to the church. We respond with feelings of anxiety and suspicion and proceed to add new security measures that will protect us. But when the church responds in this manner, what happens to the least of those Jesus spoke of? When we fail to be inclusive of all of God's people, those who may not be inside the church walls, what becomes of the oppressed, the poor, the marginalized, the victims of social injustice, the diseased and even our children? *(Luke 14:16-20; Matthew 25:31-46)*

The Bible teaches us that we are called to add ministry. Specifically, we are called to be ministers of reconciliation *(2 Corinthians 5:18-20)*. This ministry of reconciliation entails

PILLAR III: The Church

making friends of our enemies and reaching out to those who are hurting. In the process of a ministry such as this (beyond the walls), our congregations experience growth in a myriad of ways.

What shall we say of these things: Since God calls, commands and expects the local church to grow, and growth is a result of ministry beyond the walls, we must give attention to "outward focused ministry," which requires saints to be equipped, but not necessarily expect.

The emphasis of this convocation is to empower saints to tell the story of Jesus and His love for all people. Sometimes we make evangelism a complex ministry, but in essence it is very simple. It involves telling what we know about Jesus.

Additionally, we want to emphasize some challenges of ministering outside the walls. In many ways this type of ministry causes us to turn our local churches upside down. But we are reminded that there was a Jew from Galilee who did that in His day.

What we want to convey in the 16th Annual Convocation is that all of God's children have the ability to extend ministry beyond the walls. We want to give ideas and experiences that give evidence and witness to churches that are not necessarily large in numbers, but are growing because of the ministry beyond the walls. Growth is taking place within those inside the walls as they become better at loving God and neighbor and being disciples of Jesus Christ. Numerical growth is a by-product of ministry beyond the walls, and not the motivation for ministry. The motivation is simply love of God and neighbor.

No, we are not called to have large churches, but we are called to have *growing* churches. Ministry beyond the walls is not an

PILLAR III: The Church

easy call, but neither was the cross. Our theme "Beyond the Walls," challenges the Christian Methodist Episcopal Church and all of its local congregations with another question. "Do we believe God loves the world?" If we answer in the affirmative, we then are charged to find ways to be involved with God in the love of the world.

Finally, at this convocation we want to help those inside the walls see how they can be strengthened in their walk with Christ. This strength is needed in order to encounter Christ and our relationships with other Christians so that ministry can extend beyond the walls. Enabling ministers and lay persons within the church walls to reach out to those who are hurting beyond the walls requires specific attention to spiritual formation and discipleship. Those who profess a call to reach out to the least of these are challenged to first be in tune with their own spirituality. The curriculum team proposes such sessions, which will enable and empower both ministers and lay through spiritual enrichment and discipleship principles.

Permission granted Ministry Beyond the Walls
By Dr. Carmichael Crutchfield
(Reprinted from 16th Annual C.M.E. Convocation
"Ministry Workshop Beyond the Walls:" Facilitator & Convener
Information Handbook)

PILLAR IV: THE COMMUNITY

PILLAR IV: The Community

A community is defined as all of the people living in a particular section, district, or various neighborhoods that make up a city where people live together, have an interest of working together to form fellowship with families, churches, elected officials, schools, political organizations, civic organizations, fraternities, sororities, and other organizations that are committed to improving their area. When a community of organizations become united together they become a force that has power to make changes that are needed to improve, schools, city hall, county, local, state and national government.

Many communities are in need of this type of leadership. For practical purposes it seems to me the church leaders should offer the type of leadership that inspires people who live in the community, and those persons who occupy the pews on Sunday and throughout the week. The pastors of various denominations should work together, to inform the citizens on issues that are causing problems and upsetting the welfare of the total community.

There are problems in the Black community where pastors and congregations have not been forceful enough on issues such as crime, school dropouts, and lack of jobs, inadequate housing, affordable health care, food and shelter for the needy and homeless. There are civic and cultural issues as well as the need to use the church facilities for citizens, and ways to develop skills and enhance Christian education. Social, health and educational pursuits are all in arrears of community concerns. When citizens are working together toward a common goal and all of the people are on the same page to help make their community a better place for generations to come; that is when a community is at its best.

A community is at its best when families are living safely in their homes, neighborhoods are without fear of crime in the

PILLAR IV: The Community

parks, on the playground and inside schools. A community is at its best when its children's schools are attaining the highest honors awarded to a school for academic achievements in math, science, art, and sports. When high school graduation rates are at 100% and all of the students are enrolled in higher education in pursuit of their goals, a community is at its best.

A community is at its best when the family is a happy unit where all of the children are trained by their parents to understand and respect those who are in leadership positions.

"It's not what we do within the walls of the church. It's what we do when we leave the walls of the church," said Rev. Michael Pledger. It has been said that segregations are at their highest point at 11:00 a. m. on Sunday. This is the hour when the faith community comes out of their homes, neighborhoods, and drive through other neighborhoods and communities to worship their God.

From these communities of faith are all denominations worshipping their God, in homes, store fronts, community centers, well-built churches with educational buildings, stained glass windows, cushion pews, specialty designed lighting and state of the art electrical systems for the preacher and the voices of choir members to deliver the Word to worshippers for inspiration. When they go back to their communities, what are they going to do when they drive through those communities and see the harvest waiting to be harvested?

These are our brothers and sisters who are in need. Although they may not be on your membership rolls, they are people of God waiting to be harvested. If our focus was on the needs of the communities instead of the needs of our memberships,

PILLAR IV: The Community

our communities would become more unified as all denominations working together. It could be Methodist, AME, AME Zion, CME, Baptist, Church of God In Christ, Lutheran, Roman Catholic, Episcopalian, Non-denomination, or any other faith.

The Kingdom of God is wherever the people of God are! We are the people of God charged to do the work of God. Our memberships are those who are in our community trying to make ends meet. The walls are crumbling in our communities. Look around you, east, west, north and south. What do you see? Poverty, people needing jobs, street walkers, drug pushers, pimps, prostitutes, young men hustling to sell anything people will buy.

You see boarded up buildings that once stood as monuments in the Black community, showcases of outstanding restaurants where VIP gathered, schools that once graduated outstanding students that excelled in education, sports and entertainment. Some even became super stars. Beautiful homes with well-kept lawns that once housed families who were the pillars of the community, well maintained apartments and family owned businesses, neighborhood parks where young boys were trained to play baseball in the Little League. With the sponsorship of local churches and businesses, some of these outstanding boys made it to the Major Leagues.

All of these fond memories have turned into broken dreams of yester-years. In too many instances Black leadership from the pulpit have remained silent to incidents that are taking place within blocks from their churches. When the leaders of the Black community keep silent, the people will remain quiet and only speak by saying "Something needs to be done." History has a way of repeating itself, and it is the strength of the leadership in the Black community, staying focused on the

PILLAR IV: The Community

issues that caused the problems in the first place, that will be our hope.

In many cities where Blacks have assumed leadership roles as business executives, legislatures and judiciary branches of government in those cities, the tax base has decreased because of the move from the city to other towns. When a city's population decreases, and businesses leave the city, their tax base decreases. This decline causes the city to become broke. As a result of lack of financial resources, cities find it difficult to support basic services such as protecting its citizens with police and fire protection, maintaining infrastructure such as streets and sanitary services, and providing health and educational services.

When a city runs out of its financial resources, it drives the population to fight its elected officials, and citizens also fight among themselves for limited resources. When a city is broke, some of the first things that are noticeable are parks, streets, street lights, city equipment, lack of police and fire vehicles, boarded up buildings, a deserted downtown, neighborhoods with overgrown grass, weeds and trash. The leadership of the government cannot function when a city or its school system is only receiving half of its budget. A city is no stronger than its citizens.

When its people are not demanding accountability, the elected officials will become non-responsive to its citizens. Citizens should make themselves available at Council and School board meetings by asking questions and demanding answers. Citizens must understand that the elected officials are accountable to them and they must stay focused on issues that are important to city government and the school system.

The walls are crumbling in the hood.

PILLAR IV: The Community

> "When Sanballat heard that we were rebuilding the wall, he became angry and was greatly incensed. He ridiculed the Jews, and in the presence of his associates and the army of Samaria, he said, "What are those feeble Jews doing? Will they restore their wall? Will they offer sacrifices? Will they finish in a day? Can they bring the stones back to life from those heaps of rubble—burned as they are?" Tobiah the Ammonite, who was at his side, said, "What they are building—even a fox climbing up on it would break down their wall of stones!" Hear us, our God, for we are despised. Turn their insults back on their own heads. Give them over as plunder in a land of captivity. Do not cover up their guilt or blot out their sins from your sight, for they have thrown insults in the face of[b] the builders." Nehemiah 4: 1-5

Ridicule can cut deeply, causing discouragement and despair. Sanballat and Tobiah used ridicule to try to dissuade the Jews from building the wall. Instead of trading insults, however, Nehemiah prayed, and the work continued. When you are mocked for your faith or criticized for doing what you know is right, refuse to respond in the same way or to become discouraged. Tell God how you feel and remember his promise to be with you. This will give you encouragement and strength to carry on. *(Life Application Bible page 802.)*

In 2015 the Black church leadership was called to rebuild the walls in their communities. The Black church leadership was called by God to speak out on issues that were causing the Black community to become ill-informed on social, moral, political, education and finance issues. These concerns of social injustices should be included in the pastors teaching and preaching and keeping the doors of the church open 24hours/7 days a week to be the watchman, the doorkeepers, the shelter in the time of a storm, a house for the lonely, the abused wife, husband and children, the homeless, jobless and all who are searching to find themselves.

PILLAR IV: The Community

The Black pastors need to understand when they are taking on the leadership role of re-building their communities, there will be a group or groups that will ridicule every move, every plan, every house to be remodeled, every block restored, every park restored. Every school closed should become a community center for that neighborhood; for every child that drops out of school needs to become educated and find employment, for every gang that has become distrustful, they will become the hands that rebuild the walls.

We must become like Nehemiah, strong in the faith of God, knowing that God will build an army around and protect us twenty four hours a day while we are completing His plan of re-building his wall in his community, to save boys and girls, men and women by giving them the confidence so they can succeed and their lives can be turned around into positive projects and action. As leaders and pastors we must not react to all of the negative criticism what will come from the folks who are watching every move we make.

We must stay prayed up and not use our energy to fight back! God will speak to our leadership just as he spoke to Nehemiah, tell the people "I can't come down; the people got a mind to work."

Black churches must take a critical look at their mission:
- Saving Souls
- Providing spiritual leadership
- Providing food, clothing, medicine and shelter
- Providing leadership to meet with gangs and street hustlers
- Providing leadership for Town Hall Meetings
- Providing leadership on crucial issues in the community
- Providing open forums with elected officials and others

PILLAR IV: The Community

- Providing leadership with the business community
- Providing support for the schools
- Providing support for school dropouts
- Providing jobs for the poor
- Providing sponsorship for sports teams and educational organizations

The whole political, social, and economic structures of a society are largely determined by its answers to these vital issues. Indeed, how are conflicts handled between families, Federal and State governments? This is to ask, what relief is offered to people by officials elected to serve in the various branches of government?

Public officials are expected to provide funding for neighborhood improvement and promote anti-gang initiatives which allow church and non-church members to work cooperatively to take back their neighborhoods with peaceful promotions. As times have changed, such as the result of the passing of the Affordable Health Care Act, officials should provide for the rich and poor fundamental provisions for health insurance.

Currently we are witnessing more and more expressions of violence and critical events involving race and racial tension. In the news media there are frequent reports of dishonest practices uncovered by banks and mortgage companies. The one percent continues to own more of the wealth each year. The ninety-nine percent protest, but the gap between the "haves and have nots" continues to increase. All of these issues ought to be a source of concern. Those who think in terms of life purely in materialistic terms argue that people are simply trying to get all they can out of life. Such a train of thought affirms that the conduct of people is physically determined by their emotions.

PILLAR IV: The Community

Our minds become somewhat disturbed from what we see and witness, which play major roles in the decisions we make. Many of our decisions are based on negative reports and hearsay, and not from positive relationships that come from understanding the Word of God. In order to get a better understanding of the issues before us, it is imperative that a person has an open mind to digest information that comes from so many sources.

More often than not, the information has been tarnished and people are responding based upon partial truths. In order to survive the fights that come from so many sources, and not become lost in the negative world, the only hope is to pray, study, and read the information with understanding, and ask God's blessings to guide us in order to have a clear picture of the situation.

My Ministry in the Gary Community

In 1967 my family and I moved to Gary, Indiana, after residing in Springfield, OH for four years. It was an exciting and challenging to be asked by my mentor Bishop J. Claude Allen to come to Gary, Indiana and become the pastor of the great historical Israel Metropolitan C.M.E. Church. The Israel Congregation was one of the leading congregations in the Christian Methodist Episcopal and other denominations in the United States. It was founded in 1916, by a group of persons migrating from the south to better the living condition for their families. The Israel C.M.E Church's history reveals that on special occasion's town hall meetings were held there, such as the NAACP, the Urban League, various political organizations, educator organizations, and illustrious figures like Mahalia Jackson. The Rev. J. Claude Allen was the pastor of Israel C.M.E. Church during the 1930s and 1940s, and he led the membership in building the great historical facility as one of the largest church buildings in the C.M.E.

PILLAR IV: The Community

Church connection with stained glass windows and a pipe organ.

Many of the families that were migrating to Gary were immigrants of all nationalities, religions, ethnic groups, and races. Gary became a melting pot for immigrants from European nations, second generation American Immigrants from Europe, and Black Americans from the South. The present population consists mainly of second and third generations of these people. Each racial group formed their own neighborhoods.

Many of the Blacks, when they arrived in the city, I am told, wanted to know where the churches were located because they had been active in their denomination down south. It was a part of their culture to keep the faith as they journeyed to a new land. In the early stages of Gary's growth there were few denominations that were alive in meeting the peoples' spiritual, moral, physical and mental needs. These were the churches that kept activities going because the people wanted somewhere to go, and the church was that place during the week and on Sunday. It was their social functions, it was their spiritual renewal, it was their fellowship where they were able to meet back home folks who had made it to their promised land, and to be brought up to date on current news and back home news.

As the population grew among Blacks migrating to Gary seeking jobs in the Steel mills, more churches were founded and organized among others denominations. It has been reported that there are more than 400 Black congregations that are now organized in Gary, IN. None of these racial groups or church denominations maintained an open policy of inviting interracial group relationships to worship, pray, study and fellowship together. However, they do hold in group and out group prejudices by fearing almost every other group. This relationship can be evidenced by the distinct exit to suburban communities in later decades.

Racist attitudes worked against any widespread sense of neighborhood cooperation or even positive communication between races. Apathy and lack of public-spirit made it difficult for federal, city, schools, churches and social agency programs to reach people in need and make significant changes in our neighborhoods. In spite of this, Gary was the steel capital of the world, and the Mother of Northwest Indiana, giving birth to all kinds of people and businesses. These factors underlie and explain many of the social problems in Gary.

The Black neighborhoods were designated as Midtown, where most people were confined to living in substandard houses, apartments, basements and wherever people could find a room. The Midtown was a community where Blacks did own their own grocery stores, service stations, pool halls, restaurants, hotels, barber and beauty shops, funeral homes, and others types of businesses. Black churches like Israel CME played a major foundational role in being the glue of Midtown, as well as ministering to the souls of Black folks in Midtown.

In the late fifties and early sixties Gary's exodus became a growing process for the business establishments and citizens who moved to the suburbs. This allowed a major shift in the political and election process for Blacks and Mexicans to be elected to leading positions, such as Mayor Richard Gordon Hatcher, who was the first Black Mayor to be elected to a major city in the United States. Many city councilmen, judges and county offices who were elected were also Black.

The exit of whites and other races of people from major cities across the United States have created some big problems for

PILLAR IV: The Community

many cities to operate because of the loss of the tax base from businesses and property taxes. As a result, the makeup of neighborhoods dramatically changed from a peaceful quiet, working-class neighborhood; where residential properties were a showcase with beautiful lawns, sidewalks, children playing in their yards, parks and parents observing all activities.

Churches and Communities were the Talk of Town

The parents and citizens took ownership in their churches and communities. Parents knew the family next door, upstairs, down stairs, in the blocks and next streets over. In most cases mothers and fathers knew the kids in the neighborhoods and they would correct them whenever they did something wrong and reported it to their parents. A community that has strong, vital churches and schools will become the spiritual and educational glue that unites families together by teaching moral, character, education, and respect and citizen responsibilities.

Something is wrong in your neighborhood when your churches and communities are not meeting the neighborhood's needs. God is holding you responsible for what is taking place in your neighborhood. The destructive forces of failing communities are often the ones who come out of the homes, churches and schools within that community. They are not strangers from another world. These are our children, our sons, our daughters and we don't know who they are. Oh yes we do!

You are the fathers and mothers! The mother carries the child for nine months in her womb, you felt the pains as the baby grew, father felt the pains also, and became sick. Have you forgotten what Solomon said?

PILLAR IV: The Community

> "Train up a child in the way he should go: and when he is old, he will not depart from it." (Proverbs 22: 6. *King James Version*)

God has given the responsibility to parents to set guidelines and boundaries for their children. You are their first teacher. Your home is their first school. Your method of teaching determines the foundation they will need to complete their journey. Your teaching from the time the baby is conceived will determine if the child is going to be a healthy baby or a baby that will be born with many physical scars because of the life style of the mother and father. Or will the child be protected by his or her parents of not becoming exposed to sinful actions that are taken place in the neighborhoods.

There are families who participate in wild parties, drinking, smoking, using hard drugs, fighting and have disrespectful attitudes toward each other. The overuse of unkind words is often the rule for communicating with each other. Parents putting each other down by abusing, degrading each other in front of the child. Mothers telling sons he isn't going to be worth anything in life the same way their dad amounted to nothing. Saying things like, "Look at you, you can't do nothing right, always late for school, never on time, you can't do nothing right. Get out of my house I am sick and tired of you. Get out and don't come back." Nag, nag, nag! Such words are rooted in systems of abuse. Your child will be forced to leave home, join a group or gang where someone in the group will accept him or her, form a relationship and be accepted by someone who gives support and love.

Communities and neighborhoods working together will cause a whole city to change their ways of acting from negative to positive. When they show love, respect and concerns toward people leaders, pastors, educators, political leaders and parents can make a big difference in the direction your

PILLAR IV: The Community

neighborhood will go. You are the ones that are committed to helping all people reach their potential in life.

Health in today's world more than ever before has become a major concern for professionals. Medical professionals, insurances companies, politicians, clergies, educators, civil rights organizations, unions, and news media all play a major role in keeping health issues before the public.

Thus, Blacks and other minorities are the principal victims of limited access to preventive care and comprehensive health services. As a result, they suffer needlessly, prolonged illness and die earlier. The white male generally lives to collect his Social Security. The average Black male does not live to collect his Social Security. The Black population suffers and dies from heart disease, hypertension and stroke at earlier ages and in greater proportion than the majority of the population.

America has the technical competence and the resources to achieve good health for all segments of the population. Americans, as a whole, must muster the determination and will to assure that every American has access to comprehensive quality health care.

With the advent of computerization of medical records, a growing concern exists that the confidentiality of personal medical record is endangered. Certain diagnoses, such as high blood pressure, sickle cell anemia and others, may deprive poor, Black and minorities of employment and cause them to pay unnecessarily high insurance premiums. Safeguards must be instituted to maintain the confidentiality of medical and other health records.

PILLAR IV: The Community

Healthy Relationships

Healthy relationships comes from God's Church, families, schools, colleges, elected officials and community leaders working on one accord to accomplish the needs of everyone to have jobs, decent housing, health insurance, safe environment, good schools, parks and a community that is safe, 24 hours per day. These concerns are the responsibilities of the leadership of the church and community working together with the political leaders to assure them what the concerns of the people are. Certainly, our world and society are filled with many social ills. These ills are attacking the foundation of our society. I raise the question, can our society continue in the direction it is headed and remained the strong family that God has created? I don't think so.

A Word from the Lord about Community

As Paul preached many years ago, "We are troubled on every side, yet not distressed; we are perplexed, but not in despair;" (2 Corinthians 4:8 *KJV*)

Paul is expressing his personal experiences and confrontations that he encountered as he journeyed through life. Each of us has had some of the same experiences and confrontations Paul has had. We are troubled on every side, yet not distressed. Our relationship with God will lead us through any situations and help us to be stronger as we are led by God in knowing that He is able to sustain us and pick us up when we have come to the end of our ability to move forward to another level. God's relationship with us kicks in and leads us to our goals. Our relationship with God helps us accomplished our objectives.

> "We are hard pressed on every side, but not crushed; perplexed, but not in despair; persecuted, but not abandoned; struck down, but not destroyed." 2 Corinthians 4:8-9 *KJV*

PILLAR IV: The Community

How many times in each of our lives we, like Paul, can we speak without a doubt that we have been knocked down by harsh words, abused, and lied on, double-crossed? When we thought we had the position that we had applied for all, the interviews were superb, but somebody in the chain of command dropped a black ball on our security? Thank God for His relationships, we are not cast down; we are not forgotten, and we are not destroyed.

Life is filled with so many opportunities. Like Paul, don't allow your disappointments to block your goals that God has confirmed for you. While you pity yourself, God has something better waiting for you. Be strong and have courage, press toward your goals. They are reachable; you must keep your heads above water, whatever conditions you may be in. God always brings you through if you keep your relationship with Him.

"I can do all things through Christ who strengthens me." (Philippians 4:13 *NKJV*)

It is Christ who gives us the strength and all things are possible for those who believe and work daily assuming that what you believe in the Lord will come to pass. The power in the relationship with Christ is sufficient to do His will and to face the challenges that arise in attaining our commitment as we press toward our goals in life. We can do all things through Christ who strengthen us.

Of all things, get a good education, get a good job, and get a good husband or a good wife. Raise the type of children we want, cultivate the type of friends we want, get the type of home we want and live in type of neighborhood we want. Go to the type of church we want, have the type of vacation we want, and get the type of security and investments we want. The Bible said, "I can do all things through Christ who

PILLAR IV: The Community

strengthens me." All things are possible for those who believe. You must assume, you must know what you believe, and you must feel it. Believe it and see it because Jesus has promised that all things are possible for those who believe. What you believe will come into your possession. Your relationship with God puts you in a position that you cannot give up because of the trouble you see, or bury your head in the sand.

God's pastors, parents, men and women, family members and children must take a look at each other and ask this simple question: *What am I doing?* God has always inspired the pastors, men and women to stick with the Word of God. Now is the time for us to come together in the Universal Church, all denominations, and work out the situations. When God's Churches come together and call on the name of God something will happen. Yes, people will change their direction. People will confess their sins and turn their lives around.

When God's people are united together, they can change the direction of the moral erosion that is destroying the foundation of families and neighborhoods. Our community has become so preoccupied with technologies: computers, cell phones, and TV and movie productions. We will accept anything in homes, churches and schools including lack of dress codes and improper language.

Since God's Church is the only institution in the world that has a membership of all kinds of people; rich, poor, blacks, white, Jews and gentile, sick and healthy, divorce and married, gay and straight. These are the people with power that comes from repenting, praying, fasting, and tarring. They are the converts, they are the leaders, and they have been trained in the doctrine of the Church membership class. They

PILLAR IV: The Community

are baptized in the water and filled with the Holy Ghost that comes from the Lord Jesus Christ.

All they have to do is to come together just as they are with a willing spirit to do the will of God, as God has promised his people.

> "If my people, which are called by my name, shall humble themselves, and pray, and seek my face, and turn from their wicked ways; then will I hear from heaven, and will forgive their sin, and will heal their land." (2 Chronicles 7:14 *KJV*)

God promised his people that He owned a house and prepared it for all people to come, pray, and He will answer their prayers. God's Prayer House is for all people who reside in the communities and are committed to enter into the house of prayer to ask God to bring healing in the land. In those days when God appeared to Solomon, the concerns were: famine, pestilence, wars, locusts devouring the land, enemies and greedy.

Today's issues in the land include: broken family relationships, crime, drought, war, sickness, moral erosion, school dropouts, lack of quality education, lack of jobs, underemployment, lack of health insurance, inability of churches to inspire their local neighborhoods. And there seems to be more crime in those neighborhoods where Black churches are located than any other neighborhoods.

I believe God is telling us as He told Solomon in his days; it is time for churches to get their acts together. In our Black neighborhoods, you see churches of all denominations, but run-down neighborhoods with boarded up buildings, burned-out houses, buildings that are defaced with graffiti denoting gang territory, prostitution, drugs and crack houses.

PILLAR IV: The Community

From what we see, I believe that God is calling on Blacks churches, their pastors, leaders and members to come together just as Solomon asked God to make provisions for the people when they sinned. God answered with four conditions for forgiveness:

1. Humbling yourself by admitting your sin.
2. Pray to God and asking for forgiveness.
3. Seek God continually.
4. Turn from your sinful behavior.

Real repentance is a relationship with God that will last, not one that is off and on. A promise today and tonight it is broken. True repentance is more than just talk. It is more than praying for one thing and when you get it you go right back to your same way of living as if God has not done anything for you. It's time to change your way of acting as a church group or individual, nation. Following these steps will lead to forgiveness. God will answer our earnest prayers.

PILLAR IV: The Community

Mayor Karen Freeman-Wilson moved through the crowd with her Spiritual Father, Elder Carrell K. Cargle, Sr. after being sworn in as Mayor of Gary, Indiana, for her second term.

Pressed For Leadership

When a congregation or a community is pressed for leaders to fill the leadership positions of a pastor, superintendent, mayor, principal, head of school, judges, representatives, commissioners, elected officials appointed on the local, county, state and national governing bodies, they are to pray and ask God for his guidance and recommendations. The communities of faith believers need to take a positive and active stand in getting involved in the process of electing or selecting individuals to hold the various leadership positions.

> "Be strong and of good courage, for to this people you shall [a]divide as an inheritance the land which I swore to their fathers to give them. Only be strong and very courageous, that you may observe to do according to all the law which Moses My servant commanded you; do not turn from it to the right hand or to the left, that you may [b]prosper wherever you go. This Book of the Law shall not depart from your mouth, but you[c] shall meditate in it day and night, that you may observe to do according to all that is written in it. For then you will make your way prosperous, and then you will have good success." Joshua 1:6-8 *(NKJV)*

These are powerful words and instructions coming from Moses. Joshua, had worked side by side with Moses, not only was he observing Moses' leadership style he was his mentor.

PILLAR IV: The Community

And he wanted to be very successful in completing the task that had been given to him. Many leaders think that success come from giving orders, driving people, not looking out for their welfare, just trying to get the job done regardless how the people feel, or what their needs may be. Too many leaders in all walks of life strive to make themselves look good, they will step over people, stress them out; and never commend them for their works and tell them what an outstanding job they have done. They will tell everybody when making a report what they have done. They will never give the credit to what God has done and the people who worked faithfully for them to make it possible.

These kinds of people are in all sorts of leadership roles: Educators, clergies, partisans, journalists, medical practitioners, financial experts, engineers, athletic coaches, entertainers and others. These persons think that prosperity and success come from having power and influence over people's lives to move ahead. God's strategy for gaining prosperity, as He told Joshua to succeed you must:

1. Be strong and courageous because the task ahead would not be easy.
2. Obey God's law.
3. Constantly read and study the Book of the Law- God's Word.

Success comes when all of the people are working together and understand they are members of the same team. Each person may have a different page to complete, and there is one person who is in charge to lead the total project. Be strong and courageous because the task ahead will not be easy.

Too often people offer themselves for leadership positions and they don't understand what the job description is. They find themselves accepting something they are not qualified to

PILLAR IV: The Community

do. These persons, if they have the right spirit, willing attitude and learn to follow instructions that have been shared with them, show a healthy sign that they are willing to accept the responsibility to complete the challenges before them.

Success comes from understanding that anything worthwhile is going to be hard to achieve. Nothing worthwhile comes easy. Leadership roles are not easy. It's hard to lead a group when they don't want to go anywhere; who are satisfied with where they are, with what they are doing, and satisfied with the way they have done it for twenty five, thirty or fifty years.

God told Joshua the task will not be easy for you to lead the people. Joshua was Moses' assistance for forty years. He knew the captains; he knew the ground, and the desert. God appointed him to become their leader. During their journey in the desert, the Israelites accepted God's Laws. The Laws were taught to the new generation to obey God's laws so they might enter into the Promised Land. As the children grew, they were often reminded that faith and obedience to God brought victory, while unbelief and disobedience brought tragedy. When the last of the older generation had died and the new generation had become adults, the Israelites prepared to make their long awaited claim on the Promised Land.

I have seen many leaders in powerful positions work hard to make them look good and forget about the needs of the people. Joshua knew the people. He had walked with them, prayed with them, and he knew their needs and was willing to provide for them. He knew their parents, grandparents; the older generation and the younger generation and what their desires were. He knew some of the issues of the older generations, who often complained about what they left behind in their home town where they grew up and started

PILLAR IV: The Community

their families. Now they are out in the desert, where the living conditions are terrible!

In my responsibilities as a Pastor and Presiding Elder, my leadership role placed me in many positions where I had to take the time to pray, look and examine the situations to help me to understand what was going on in front of my eyes. Often when I would stop my car and go into the corner store, I had to walk through a crowd of men standing on the corner in order to enter into the store to purchase what I wanted. I would always speak to the gentlemen and sometimes they would speak to me.

Sometimes I would strike up a conversation. "How are you doing?" Some would say "fine," others would say that things are tough, they need a job, a place to stay, food to eat or some would remark, "It's rough out here on the streets." Once there was a young man who was smoking marijuana. I asked him, "Why are you smoking pot?" He answered by explaining that it made him feel good, alert, important, overcome issues and circumstances that surrounded him daily. He said that it gave him a jump start with energy that would help him get things done better today than yesterday. The conversations would go and on, and I listened to their stories. Some were brought up in the church by their parents or relatives, and they were very active. I would ask what happened to you and the church. *I moved across town, no transportation to get to church, keep promising myself next Sunday, I promised myself on the next Sunday nothing would stop me from going to church. The next Sunday came and nothing changed. I was out of it and each Sunday was just like all the other ones. I was lost and out of touch.*

When you are out of touch with reality, you are living in a dark world. You want to get out of it and tell yourself you are going to, but something on inside keeps telling you this is the best place for you. You have made lots of friends. They are your brothers and sisters and you are now glued together. That's the story of so many who have chosen the homeless street life style. Some drop out of school, some left home, and some left their families, wives, girlfriends and children. Having lost their jobs and no benefits there's nothing to do but stand on the corners all day. They all admitted that it was much better to have a place to stay than to stand on the corners trying to find a place to keep warm and something to eat.

They reminded me of the Israelites complaining they would prefer staying in their land instead of journeying into a strange land looking for a dwelling place. Some of these men wanted to go back home to join their families, but because of the fears and lifestyles on drugs, stealing, dirty bodies that needed medical attention, they were afraid to try.

They had lost hope and faith in themselves to survive with a family. Some of these persons are very gifted and smart; they just got caught with the wrong groups that had more influence over them than their family members. If they had kept a relationship with God, their wives, and children as they have formed with their street friends, their whole life in the sight of God and their community would be a blessing to all.

There are Black males who have drifted too far from the Promised Land where their foundations were built by their fathers, mothers, grandparents, great grandparents, uncle, aunts, and relatives, men of the church and communities that feared God. These Black men were strong soldiers who fought in the trenches, in the fields, share cropping on the farm land working from sun up to sun down. Praying as they took care of their routine, that their children will not have to go through some of the roads of hard time they had to journey through.

PILLAR IV: The Community

It was the father teaching to their sons, men were the men of the house; the backbone, the protector, the provider, the enforcer of the rules in the home. Fathers taught their sons how to work, no matter what the tasks were, they were taught to do it with dignity by making it the best job anywhere. They were taught to do their best in whatever they chose, in the fields, in schools, in the church and their family. *You are the bread maker, respect yourself, your family, your community and be strong men and fathers, stand tall with your head up, don't walk with your head down, look up and see fields and opportunity before you.*

In this generation there are so many people who are standing on the sidelines or street corners gazing up at the sun, stars and moon. Yet the question is: what are we willing to do? Are we part of the problem or the solution? You can journey through many communities where the un-employment rates are so high and Black men are standing on the corners looking, hustling and watching the world go by. Many of these men want to work, but jobs are not available. Some are not able to find a job because they have no job skills. Others have fallen through the cracks because they dropped out of school, arrested and served prison time. And others without a foundation from a home where a dad was in charge and a mother were there to enforce the rules.

Business in the Community

Many years ago while living on the farm, there lived a farmer down the road from us. This man farmed many acres of cotton and corn. At certain seasons of the year he would send his trucks in town to pick up workers who were waiting at the market place to be hired. I am told there were hundreds of persons always waiting to be hired. The truck only could accommodate fifty people; the first fifty who got on the truck were taken to the farm, while others were left there. This was

PILLAR IV: The Community

a day to day procedure until harvest was completed for that season, and the harvesting of the cotton and corn was ready.

I am told throughout America this was the practice for many farmers and construction companies to go into the city looking for day workers. There were always plenty of day workers standing on corners waiting to be hired. Even today there are people who are standing on certain corners in many Black communities, some are looking for work, others for a hand out and some nothing to do but stand there on the corners talking about what they used to do. Some are capable of holding a job; they just need a little push and help to identify what their strengths and weaknesses are.

In the parable of the workers in the vineyard (Matthew 20:1-16 (*NIV*)), it tells about workers who were hired for a certain amount per day, and not by hourly wages. The owner agreed to pay those who were first picked up and hired from the market place at different hours.

In the payment, the judgment of the house holder is vindicated. These last were paid first, and out of the goodness of the householder, each one received a full day's pay.

The goodness of the householder overcame them. They were amazed at his generosity, those who were hired first supposed that they were going to receive far more than the contract called for, but the householder, faithful to his contract, paid them exactly what he promised. He kept his word to the dot and the letter. These early workers then broke out into open rebellion. They murmured against him, not because he did not live up to his contract, but because they did not get more than the contract called for. This showed them up for what they were. They were looking at the possibility of exploiting him.

PILLAR IV: The Community

They raised a grudge against him because he was generous to others. The householder kept his contract with them, and had a right to give generously to others if he so desired. Because of the difference in their spirit, that last were made first and the first were made last.

Jesus seeks permanent servants to honor Him, men and women who love the work and who are not in His service for pay or reward. We are not to work for the Lord by contract, or the reward, for what we can get out of it. We are to work for our Savior just for the love of the Lord and we are to leave the reward up to Him. There are some who labor in the vineyard of Christ for what they can get out of it; performance in denominational office, commendation from the members of the church, political advancement, love of power and praise, love of prestige and fame.

These get what they contracted for. If the soloist sings in order to be commended of men, when the commendation is said, the contract has been fulfilled. But Christ seeks workers who labor not for fame or commendation or earthly reward, but just for the love of the Savior. We are not to seek big and handsome places ourselves, but we are to seek only to do Gods will in the earth. If it is a little place God chooses for us, we are to be happy in it and do our best by it.

> Where shall I work, today, dear Lord?
> And my love flowed warm and free.
> Then the Lord pointed out a tiny place
> And said, "Tend that for me."
> I cried, "Oh, no, not over there,
> Why, no one would ever see,
> No matter how well my work was done.
> Not that little place for me.
> When the Lord spoke, He was not harsh.
> He answered me tenderly:
> "Tell me, precious child of mine,

PILLAR IV: The Community

> Are you working for them or for me?
> Nazareth was a little place
> And so was Galilee."
>
> Author Unknown

The rewards of God are not according to what men think is their merit. Nor is it in terms of material possessions. The rewards of God are arbitrary.

As a race we spend so much time quarreling among ourselves. We need to look at the vastness of the world, and in our community and see the greatness of God, instead of working so hard blocking our brothers and sisters from getting some of the help they need. We need to help each other when you know that your brothers and sisters are in need of help. Their children are struggling in school and you know it, instead of helping you come up with all types of excuses why you can't do this, and why you won't do that. It is by the grace of God that you and your children are not in the same situations.

Be careful how you look at people in your family, your neighborhoods and those who are in your social group. We need to come together as families, social groups, working together to change the social ills that are hindering progress in our families and communities. We have the know-how, the expertise and skills to change our communities that are short of determination.

As a Black race that contributed so much to the America lifestyle less than 175 years ago, our grand, great, and great-great grandparents helped build this country from it foundation to where it is today. Our forefathers helped build the economy, bridges, roads, hospitals, government buildings, mansions, schools, parks, lakes and temples. They were the strong arms, hands, eyes and ears to do the works that machines are doing today. These fathers were engineers,

PILLAR IV: The Community

carpenters, plumbers and welders. They were the strong connection that kept the buildings going up to its highest points. They worked from sun up to sun down, not getting paid; just a place to sleep and eat.

We must become stronger today than ever before if we are going to be the race that will help this nation to come its fullest and true meaning that all people are created equally in the sight of God. I believed that God has called the Black race to be on guard 7 days a week and 24 hours a day in order to achieve all of the opportunities in education, sports, politics, business, entertaining, finance, and religion. The fact is that everything Blacks participated in, they rise to the top in those areas. Yes, to the top.

We must become smarter in every area by empowering our children to excel in all studies and use the gifts that God has blessed them with. We can no longer stand on the sideline watching other races succeed in building strong communities and neighborhoods where there are businesses, banks, cultural centers and churches and schools working together. We must come together and help families stabilize their community, to become free of crime, drugs, gangs, prostitution, and other distrustful forces that have caused so many families to lose their sons and daughters in violent actions of crime in too many of our communities.

It is a proven fact that the Black race is capable of excelling in all fields, when given the opportunities. For years blacks were denied participation in all major sports, politics, entertainment; all professions, engineers, scientist, math, medical, law, finance, and denied attendance to the best high schools, colleges and universities all because we were Black. Blacks didn't allow segregation to block them from excelling in the gifts that God had given them from their birth. Let's take a critical look at some of the profession where Blacks

PILLAR IV: The Community

broke the color line. As I have stated above in each one of the professions there were obstacles, racism, threats, bombings, rioting to prevent people from succeeding. Through it all, God chose the right persons. When God chooses, no group can stop; once the person or persons have proven themselves they were there to make contributions for the good of all races of people. Those who were in sports began to hit home runs, make sensational plays, touch downs, broke records in running, boxing. Those in politics, finance, legal, medicine graduating from some of the best schools in the world excelled. Thank God for the support that families and communities gave in knocking the wall of resistance down. Once it was proven that success comes in many colors the doors of resistance were opened.

However, the first who opened the doors always encounter resistance. That was seen when President Obama served as the first Black President of the United States, and racism showed its very ugly face while he tried to move this country in a better direction. It has been said President Obama was the first president in many years to receive fifty-two percent of the votes cast in both of his elections. It is hoped the next Black elected president will not have to go through the testing and proving ability that President Obama had to endure.

Now is the time for all races of people to work together and accomplish their goals of getting a good education, finding the jobs they have prepared themselves for, be able to move into the type of neighborhood they can afford, where there is peace, goodwill for all people to have the opportunity to enjoy the parks and neighborhoods where there is no crime. Their children will have the opportunity to attend and graduate from the best school systems in the world, while preparing them to attend the best colleges and universities in the world, and expect to find good jobs that will pay well after graduation.

PILLAR IV: The Community

Blacks and other minorities are to remember you have to achieve and be smarter than others in order to get the jobs you seek. This is not to the time to give up and make excuses that somebody else always steps in front of you and gets the job you are seeking.

Education is the most powerful tools your can have. "If you don't have it, make sure you get it. Once you get it, make sure you use it. If you don't use it, you will lose it."

Black fathers had a gift from God in how they shared their experiences by related them in a timely way with their children that had a great impact on what they were teaching. "It's more in the man than it is in the land." 'There were two farmers who both had four acres of land. One planted cotton seeds, corn and green beans; and when harvest time came; he harvested one and a half bales of cotton, five bushels of corn and two baskets of green beans.

The other man planted the same seeds on his four acres of land. When harvest time came, he harvested two and a half bales of cotton, ten bushels of corn, and ten baskets of green beans. One man knew how to till the ground, when to plant, when to water, when to fertilize his ground and when to weed out the grass. The other man who harvested less from his four acres didn't know how to attend to what he had planted. You see, "It's more in the man than it is the land."

The Black fathers knew that the father was the glue that kept the family together. And he was determined to keep his family together by using everything within his power by seeking jobs in his community, or going across the state line, or wherever jobs were available. In many instances where the father would relocate that would cause him to leave his family until he secured a job and place for them to stay.

Sometimes this would take several months before the fathers could send for his family. In many situations when the family would relocate from one community culture to another community culture, it would create an adjustment problem for his family; especially with his sons. Living within a new community always brings in some new experiences of socializing, joining a new church, enrolling the children in schools, and the pressure from peer groups and gang activities. Because of the father's hands-on relationship with his children; sharing with them and spending quality time with them daily, by going to the parks, sport events and eating out together as a family, it enabled the family to reconnect from the time it took the father to find a job and housing, to moving his family. Once the family became adjusted in their neighborhood, involved in church, school and community activities which led them to meet new friends, and develop new pathways of finding their future and goals in life, it enabled them to become successful in life.

> "The education pipeline leads directly to the doors of industry and business, so it only makes sense for us to pay attention to the quality of what goes into that pipeline in a child's early years and do what we can to ensure that the young adults who come out are prepared to join a quality workforce."
> Blake Wilson, President, Mississippi Economic Council.

I must agree with Blake Wilson, in my opinion, it is never too late to restore a broken relationship. It is better to restore than to drift farther and farther apart. If it is never too late to repent to God, we must be willing to repent and forgive one another. This gesture symbolizes to God a willingness on our behalf to give our lives to God.

PILLAR IV: The Community

Community Involvement
Without a vision the people perish!

The unified church leadership of all faith groups working together to accomplish their visions of helping citizens understand how to overcome and resolve their daily problems. It is imperative that the people understand the visions. The vision must be clear and understandable for people. When they see it, they will buy into it and become supporters on fire to accomplish the goals. This happened when Senior Bishops of the AME, AME Zion and CME met after hearing of the crises in Ferguson, Missouri. "Black Life Matters" and the Senior Bishops of three major Black Methodist denominations issued a pastoral call to their denomination in a joint effort to form a working agenda with key leaders of each denomination:

> ➤ Work One, Northwest Indiana Workforce Board, Inc. and Gary Education Leadership Council Blueprint for Educational and Workforce Success:

PILLAR IV: The Community

- ➤ Work One Northwest Indiana Workforce Board, Inc. and Gary Community School Corporation
- ➤ Gary Education Leadership Council Creating a Blueprint For Educational and Workforce Success
- ➤ A Multiple Education Pathways Project Funded by the US Department of Labor

The Community Education Network Committee is charge with:

- Participating in creation of an asset map of programs for, and in support of, educational pathways operating currently
- Reviewing gap analysis of High School Renewal Committee
- Reviewing national best practices & identification of new strategies for consideration for local pathways
- Identification of barriers to opportunities for integration with School Corporation
- Identification of barriers that prevent students from continuing their education
- Finding and expanding local pathways between secondary and post-secondary education
- Creation of draft actions for consideration by full Leadership Council

In order to complete the initial phases of this, the committee reviewed national best practices, met with representatives of local institutions, identified barriers experienced by students pursuing post-secondary education and training, and proposed initial strategies as the basis for new pathways.

Major Sources and Resources utilized
- Interview with Work One Staff, Gary
- Interview with principals, counselors, and administrator from Gary Community School Corporation

PILLAR IV: The Community

- Open Meadows program, Portland Oregon
- Fast Forward Center, Sinclair Community College, Dayton, Ohio
- Pathways to College, Chicago, Illinois
- MEP Asset of Services for Out-of- School Youth

Current Pathways

There are three routes to post-secondary education:
- Traditional: High School to University/Community College/Training
- Non- Traditional: GED/ABE to University/Community College/Training
- Non- Traditional: Dropout to GED/ABE to University/Community College/Training

Young people in Gary encounter a number of barriers regardless of which of the three pathways they may take. Those taking a non- traditional route, however, encounter many more barriers. The most common barriers have been identified and are included below:

Current pathways to degrees/certification include the following:
- Regular admission, or
- Guided studies at Indiana University which may include some targeted work in Math or Language, or
- Remedial programs available at Ivy Tech.

Reports indicate that a large percentage of students entering Ivy Tech are involved in some remedial programs. This appears to be particularly true of those who enter through one of the non- traditional pathways.

All of the best practice programs that were reviewed offered one-stop programs for out of school youth. That is to say multiple services are available through a single contact and most often in a single location. GED/ABE services are offered, remedial programs are available and student support can be obtained on site.

Many of the programs offer dual enrollment/dual credit and take place on-site at local community colleges.

Conclusions and Recommendations
The committee has several general points on concurrence.
- Students prefer and need relationships in a small class format.
- Employers prefer a diploma over a GED
- Fast track and other programs in cooperation between schools and Ivy Tech allow students to receive dual credit and should be encouraged.
- Students need access to information through a single phone call or a single office visit.
- Traditional practices are not working; we have to do something different.
- This committee and this council must have the courage to make hard recommendations for change.

The following lists the major barriers students experience and the committee's suggested strategies to overcome them. Future work will involve identifying resources and partners.

Barrier: Distance from education
Strategy:
- Outreach
- Refresher courses/remediation
- Career Counseling
- User-friendly environment

Barrier: Lack of information/Outreach
Strategy:
- Improved communication and materials

PILLAR IV: The Community

- Use of outreach workers
- Central/ single phone number
- Central location for information and services
- Career information at GRD/ABE sites
- Case management

Barrier: Inadequate preparation
Strategy:
- Improve career exposure in High School
- GED prep classes with teacher involvement to supplement computer programs
- Improved communication between secondary schools regarding course requirements
- Tutoring
- Testing preparation for students who've been out of the system for some time

Barrier: Cost
Strategy:
- Access to information
- Outreach
- Programs that combine work & education
- Stipends
- Courses with flexible hours to accommodate work schedule

Barrier: Personal Circumstances
Strategy:
- Case management services
- Support services available on site
- Improved communication between support service providers & education providers

Barrier: Failure to pass GQE
Strategy:
- Improved outreach to target population

- Availability of tutoring
- Information about options

Barrier: Lack of positive support
Strategy:
- Improved availability of mentors
- Access to peer support
- Case management
- Incentives
- Positive attitude of teachers/counselors

Barrier: Transportation
Strategy:
- Improve coordination with city bus services
- Support for carpools
- One stops

Barrier: Communication/ Access
Strategy:
- Improved outreach
- Improved case management & follow- up   65
- Website
- Adequate staffing
- Staff training

Barrier: Disconnect from School to Work to Life
Strategy:
- Earlier career planning exposure within the schools
- Career exposure/planning in all GED/ABE
- Availability of Work One liaison at adult based-education GED sites

Next Steps
- Further research on Best Practices

PILLAR IV: The Community

- Additional data collection: remedial education; GED and post –secondary admission; others
- Further exploration of dual enrollment opportunities
- Possible Task Team to refine selected models
- Identification of resources and partners
- Development of appropriates pathways for inclusion in Blueprint

(Multiple Education Pathways Community Education Network Committee Summary Report July 18, 2008)

The Flow of Business Economics
Community is the place where success flows. Together, as one for the good of the Universe
The components are dependent upon one another. The money from one is what fuels the life of the other.

PILLAR IV: The Community

I'm Making A positive Difference in Gary, Indiana

(Recite Daily using your city's name)

➤ I will no longer stand idly by while the media and others speak negatively about my community.

I'm MAD. I'm making a positive difference in _____

➤ I will no longer refer to Gary, Indiana as the crime capital of America.

I'm MAD. I'm making a positive difference in _____

➤ My property will beautify the community and if I don't own any property I will buy some abandoned property and renovate it.

I'm MAD. I'm Making A positive Difference in _____

➤ The more property that I own, the greater my net worth and the contributions I make to the city's economy through paying my property taxes.

I'M MAD. I'm making a positive difference in _____

➤ I will seize the opportunities for growth and prosperity that are ripe within my community.

I'm MAD. I'm making a positive difference in _____

➤ I will stay committed and remain hopeful about the economic revitalization for my community.

I'm MAD. I'm making a positive difference in _____

➤ I will continue to pray and completely trust God for the spiritual, economic, social, and positive transformation for my community.

I'm MAD. I'm making a positive difference in _____

➤ Gary, IN. is a community that breeds greatness, excellence, success, and wealth.

I'm MAD. I'm making a positive difference in _____

I'm MAD. I (state your name) _____ am making a positive difference in _____ today, tomorrow, and forever.

Written by Carla J. Cargle, copyright 2008,
www.thefinancialtruth.com

PILLAR IV: The Community

Says racial hang ups hang on
By Vernon A Williams, Post Tribune Staff Reporter 1974

The Rev. Carrell K. Cargle, President of the Urban League of Northwest Indiana, says racial polarization is as much a problem as ever socially and economically.

"The suburban migration of whites has to be halted for the continued well–being of urban areas in Northwest Indiana," the Rev. Cargle asserted.

His remarks came during a speech at the Urban League's second annual "President's Luncheon" at the Downtown Gary Holiday Inn Friday.

In his address, the Rev Cargle reviewed the Urban League's accomplishments in 1974 and outline goals for this year.

The Luncheon, attended by business and civic officials, was designed to give the public an idea of what the League is all about. The Rev Cargle lashed out at racism he said is still all too prevalent in Northwest Indiana.

He said there was no other logical explanation for the suburban migration of whites from the cities in the area. "Unfortunately, residency in Gary is often for employment purposes and not by choice and the added effect of the suburban migration is working against community cooperation," the Rev Cargle said.

"Though some 280 persons were placed in jobs as the result of League's efforts in 1974, an increasing cooperation from area businesses is needed to the city's seven to 12 per cent unemployment rate," the Rev Cargle added. He said, "Business and industry must work to strengthen the family ties of our community and upgrade the economy."

The Rev. Cargle also said educational needs of the Gary area were paramount last year and will remain a vital issue in 1975. "The Urban League believes schools should be both responsible and responsive to the public and we are urging the formation of a regular workshop among parents, teachers, administrators and students to eliminate some of the apathy surrounding the education of youth," he said.

Under the provisions of the Emergency School Act Program, funded by the Department of Health, Education and Welfare (HUD) through Title 7, the league sponsored a tutorial and cultural enrichment course on Saturdays for students from grades four to six at Indiana University

PILLAR IV: The Community

Northwest. The tutorial emphasis was put on math and reading. Some 125 students now participate in this program.

The Rev Cargle said the Urban League was also active in concerns of housing, consumer affairs, criminal justice, and various other community services last year.

The League staff spent a minimum of 12 hours weekly servicing other social help agencies such as Metro Corps, the Lake County Children Home, Boy Council, and the Indiana Sickle Cell Anemia Foundation, The Rev. Cargle added.

He said the Urban League of North West Indiana is in its 30th year, couldn't have made such accomplishments as those noted in his address had it not been for the Lake Area United Way with which his organization is affiliated.

The Rev. Cargle pledged the Urban League's support for all individuals and agencies working to better Gary and said in closing, "Mother Gary was founded on a rock of sand and steel was nursed by the waters of Lake Michigan and gave birth too many. She must live."

Connecting the Future with the Past

The visions of any community can become true when all of the people come together on the same page working faithfully until dreams have become a reality. All things are possible when families, schools, churches and community leadership teams unite their efforts by coming together as one, and the community's politicians unite together to make all things possible.

The Midwest has something to shout about! Let's take a look where we were in 2015, and look back over one hundred years and see some of the major historical developmental sites that stand as a monument for the future, connecting the future with the past. The past we see Indiana Dunes, Marquette Park, Gary, the Steel Capital of the World, the Old Pullman Neighborhood that built Pullman cars in the south end of Chicago, where President Barack Obama has designated the Pullman Neighborhood as a National Historic

PILLAR IV: The Community

District and National Park. The President's Committee selected President Barack Obama Library to be built on the south side of Chicago, near the University of Chicago in one of the proposed parks known as Jackson or Washington.

Gary, Indiana was known as The Steel Capital of the World and attracted immigrants from all over the world, and from the states of Alabama, Mississippi, Arkansas, and Georgia, to seek jobs in order to better their living conditions. Today we look to the future and see the building of Michael Jackson and Jackson Five Museum in Gary, Indiana, where thousands of travelers visit 2300 Jackson Street each year just to see his birth place, and another attraction to see when the future National Civil Rights Hall is built.

What attractions they all will bring to Gary, Northwest Indiana and Chicagoland as they travel east and west, north and south on interstates Highways 94/80, I65, toll road I90, and the Gary/ Chicago Metropolitan Airport! What an attraction it will become when leadership teams use their resources and expertise to make this area a financial jewel where thousands of people are hired and billions of dollars will flow into the economy through building hotels, restaurants, car rentals, theater centers and vendors to accommodate the tourist attractions, that will be visiting President Obama's Presidential Library, Pullman National Park, Miller Beach and the Indiana National Dunes. This will be possible when families, schools, churches, communities and politicians come together to achieve workable goals that are profitable for all.

This vision can become true when all of the people and financial institutions come together and get on the same page, working faithfully until this dream has become a reality. All things are possible when families, schools, churches and community leadership teams unite their efforts by coming together as one to make all things possible.

PILLAR IV: The Community

What Happens When God's People Come Together?
The Glory of God returns to the communities and churches, religious leaders, political leaders, educational leaders, civic leaders and key persons with the know how to accomplish goals without giving up. When people are involved in education, arts, theater and mentoring programs that broaden their scopes of understanding relationships through workshops, love feasts, revivals, true confessions powerful Bible studies, powerful preaching, teaching, worshiping, great music, powerful singing, members showing love toward each other, friendly attitudes toward visitors, strangers, sinners, the homeless and rejects are welcome.

If these spiritual points are adhered to in the church, the communities will become a driving force that will enable them to accomplish their needs of rebuilding family structure, financial goals, shopping centers , housing markets for its people, schools for its citizens, jobs, a city free of crimes, good police and fire departments, and a strong business community that works for all of its citizens. It has been said

PILLAR IV: The Community

by some writers that we, as historical Black churches, don't show enough concern for our people and the communities where our churches are located. We see daily the activities that are taking place in our community and we only give lip service to what needs to be done.

Each week, month and year the problems become out of control and our people become less interested in their churches and communities. As a result, too many of our children are dropping out of schools, dropping out of Sunday Schools, character building programs; babies are having babies. Too many of the Black fathers and boys are incarcerated. Black women and Black girls are having more problems finding soul brothers to relate to.

Too many parents, churches and faith based organizations are not supporting their schools and community in their projects. It's time for churches and community leadership to raise the standard bar for our children. Standing on corners begging for money to help in their school projects to buy uniforms, band instruments, church projects sends a negative message to our children that they have to beg to get what they want. We as pastors and community leaders must do a better job of teaching our people about stewardship.

Inspiring Past for a Better Future

Many Blacks have pulled themselves up by their boot straps. They paid the price of hard knocks, racial prejudices, and negative environment. And through it all they broke the color lines, in schools, music, theatre, art, sports, entertainment, politics, religion, business, medicine, and many other professions. It was because of their faithfulness and prayers of faithful mothers, fathers and saints who prayed daily on their knees and around altars on Sunday mornings when the pastors would call the role of those persons who were on the firing line of breaking the walls of segregation.

PILLAR IV: The Community

I can recall my mother and father calling the names of persons who were involved in a boxing match. I can remember Joe Lewis fought Max Shilling, and became the world heavy weight champion of the world. We would go to the general grocery store to listen to the fight on the general store radio. Jackie Robinson broke the color line in baseball; Dr. Carter G. Woodson received his Doctor of Philosophy degree in American History from Harvard University 1912. (Dr. Woodson was the founder of Negro History Month; February 1915)

"The Negro and the American Stage," by Alain Locke highlights the careers of several prominent persons within our culture. Josephine Baker began her career as an end girl in the chorus line of Negro musical hits of the early Twenties such as "Shuffle Along" (1921), and "The Chocolate Dandies" (1924); Bill Robinson was a jazz singer and great entertainer. Dr. Daniel H. Williams, a charter member of the American College of Surgeons discovered a way to "sew up" the heart; and Dr. Charles R. Drew developed the blood plasma theory and the blood bank that saved countless lives.

There are so many in all fields as I have mentioned who attended or graduated from colleges and universities, establishing scholarships, cultural centers in their names that help students to improve in their quest for knowledge and establishing businesses. Today, noted figures have caught the spirit of helping their Black communities such as Magic Johnson, Oprah Winfrey, Tyler Perry, John Cain and other celebrities.

Economic Concerns
What is so disturbing to me is the fact that sometimes when I read in the newspapers there are high paying jobs that are available in the community for qualified workers who are skilled and certified electricians, engineers, computer experts

PILLAR IV: The Community

and heavy duty operators. Many of these jobs that are available for work is for local, city, county, state and federal government projects; like road construction, schools, airports, bridges, building repairs, hospitals, sewer lines, and interstate highways contracts. It seems to me the citizens of black leadership should demand that the schools of the city, states include courses in their curriculum that will prepare and qualify students for those available jobs.

Full employment for all citizens should be a goal to be met on all levels: local, county, state and federal. The churches and citizens must play a major role by working with unions, National Urban League, NAACP, and elected officials to establish a national policy that all citizens be guaranteed a job commensurate with their skills.

Unemployment rates among Black males is at 14.2%; among white males 6.8%; Black female 12.1% and among white females 6.2% .However, In many of the urban centers ,like Gary, IN, Detroit, MI, Cleveland , OH, Chicago, IL, Washington, D.C. and others, the rates are much higher among Blacks. (Jobs: The State of Black America, National Urban League)

The experiences of churches, Urban League, and NAACP involvement through job training and outreach programs have shown that a team effort will improve the economic and social benefits when the communities are working together for the total economy and federal expenditures for employment programs. Blacks and poor families must not be made the victims of benign neglect. In a period of high disproportions, burdens are being placed upon those who need help the most.

It is imperative for us to recognize that no family in America need to go through some of the same struggles their parents had to go through in order to find a job for qualified workers.

Many students enter college because their parents expect them to. Many don't know what they want; they just go to college because it is a demand that comes from their parents. It may be wise for children to take placement entrance exams to determine their interest and talents. I have seen many students graduate from college and discover their major was not what they wanted. As a result too many finish with four year college degrees and no job, student loans to pay, and they end up back home with mother and father. This can cause a hardship between both parents and children.

Crime and Justice
Observations made in "The Assassination of the Black Male Image" by Earl Ofari Hutchinson and the "New Jim Crow" by Michelle Alexander suggests that the high volume of crime and black incarceration are more systemic rather that coincidental within black America.

I want to take a critical look at some of the causes of crime in our community. You may not agree with what I am going to say. As I have mentioned in Chapter One, The Family Pillar, father and mother are the glue that holds the family together. They are the first teachers that prepare their children for school, because the home is their children's first school.

The parents build the foundation before the child is born and when the child arrives they continue the process of teaching Biblical principles, how to pray their first prayer *("Lord lay me down to sleep, I pray the Lord my soul will keep, if I should die before I wake I pray the Lord my soul will keep, Lord bless dad, mommy and everybody. Amen.")* This was a universal prayer that was learned by children before they could make a complete sentence.

One of the major problems in the black community since the early fifties has been the problem of broken relationships. A

PILLAR IV: The Community

home without a father, single-parent families, out of wedlock births, drug abuse, abused mothers living in frustration because the father of the child or children cannot be located. Now there are many of the mothers and fathers are children from a broken relationship.

For some single mothers their frustration seems to affect their children as a result of not seeing a father image in the home. Sometimes the mother is so frustrated she neglects to show any love toward her children. When no love is shown in the home, the child or children will withdraw and find love on the streets, in gangs, and in homes where an attachment of a relationship is formed. It has been stated in several findings by sociologists that the major problems in the Black community today stem from babies born out of wedlock; more than 60 - 70 percent of all babies born in the Black community. What does this have to do with it? The answer is simple, raising a family without a father image or his influence in the home, has contributed to the breakdown of family relationships.

As a result there is no male voice that speaks with authority; no enforcements of rules and regulations have contributed to rising crime in the Black community.

However, as I have mentioned before, I know of many cases where a single mother has done a superb job in raising her family; a single mother with a strong constitution and determination that her child is not going to get caught in gang activities. Many single mothers kept their children involved in structural and supervised activities that included going to the library daily and reading books that were motivating the child; keeping a ledger of what they read.

These programs will enrich the children's lives, and they will become so engaged and love what they are doing. It has been

PILLAR IV: The Community

proven when children are involved in character building programs, their minds become adjusted and programmed to what they are involved with. Well rounded programs will not allow them to get involved in negative activities. In the Black communities crime is present from sun up to sun down seemingly by design.

Black people want change. Some of the changes they make involve moving out of the neighborhood, or changing the school their children are enrolled in. After relocating into a different community they soon discover the same problems are reoccurring. What are the problems? The problem is Black on Black crime. I strongly believe when the Black pastors and God's congregations, political leaders, professional people, business owners, educators, unions and community leaders come together and make a movement toward change, the ceasing of all crimes in their communities will occur by the appropriation of services, .

This must be a God-fearing movement, with Black men and Black women who are not afraid to stand on God's firing line. With leaders in the community coming together and bringing their expertise to God's table sharing what is needed to improve the quality of life in the Black community, these things will occur:

1. Strong Family ties
2. Training people for the job market; how to apply and how to keep a job.
3. Reduce and prevent crime through citizens' initiatives and involvement.
4. Work with the police and the criminal justice systems to make it more responsive to the needs of the Black communities.
5. Provide services to the victims of crime.

PILLAR IV: The Community

6. Encourage businesses and industries to hire the ex-offender, the addict and the undesirable.
7. Educating the general public about its role in the crime prevention process.
8. Help develop systems for the criminal justice system to make it more responsive to the needs of local citizens.
9. Demand that persons who are incarcerated become involved in a curriculum that will help them to prepare for the job market when they are released.

Again, I raise the question, "Why is crime so high in the Black community?" Because we allow it!

Why crime is so high in the Black community? The answer for us may seem complex but it is really uncomplicated. It's because of the family breakdown within our community!

The Black race has been the major contributors in helping white people relocate into new communities to build new homes and new churches, because we are buying their old homes and old churches. In many instances we have to make major improvements on the homes and church buildings before moving into the properties. For many Black families this is a dream to be able to move in to a new community that is much better than the old. The Black race has been a major contributor to the financial and business communities for many years. It is about time for the Black communities, with all of their resources and expertise in all professions to invest in their communities in order to stabilize the Black race and their communities as other races have done.

PILLAR IV: The Community

When People's Voices are Heard

Throughout neighborhoods, communities, towns, cities, states, United States and the world when the people register their protest through writing, and demonstrating, their opinions will be heard and their goals will be met. Take notice of what has happened since 1862:

1. Emancipation Proclamation issued by President Lincoln
2. Integration of schools and Public Accommodations became the law of the land.
3. United Arm Forces Services Integrated
4. Communities became safer.
5. Schools curriculums improved
6. Hospitals met the needs of the people.
7. Unions integrated.
8. Elected officials became more accountable.
9. Civil Rights Bills became the law of the land
10. All children enrolled in school.
11. Black Lives Matter

PILLAR IV: The Community

The Glory of God returned to the people in their leadership roles: religious leaders, civic leaders and key persons with know-how, to accomplish goals without giving up. When people are involved in their educational pursuit of mentoring, developing programs to broadening their scope of understanding relationships through workshops, love feasts, revivals, true confessions, powerful Bible studies, powerful preaching, teaching, worshipping, powerful singing, members showing love toward each other, friendly attitudes toward visitors, strangers, sinners, homeless, rejects and all of the creations of God.

If these spiritual points are adhered to and taught in families, schools, churches and communities, those will become driving forces that enable people to accomplish their goals of rebuilding family structures, improve financial goals, improving housing for its people, better schools for its citizens, jobs, city free of crimes, good police and fire departments, and a strong business community that works for all of its citizens.

PILLAR IV: The Community

When People Come Together
1. Changes come for the betterment of the community.
2. Specific projects will be accomplished.
3. Plans of action will attract people.
4. The people will become united.
5. The citizens of all communities work together: local, state, national and international will accomplish their goals.
6. Gary, Northwest Indiana and the Midwest want a Jackson Five Entertainment Arts Museum Complex in Gary, IN. It will happen because the people will become united and their voices will fight for what they want.
7. If the people of Gary, Northwest Indiana and the United States want a Black Civil Rights National Hall of Fame they will get it because of the leadership team and the people want it.
8. There is power when individuals are united and working together on the same goals.

PILLAR IV: The Community

9. When the leaders of communities work together and respect each other without forming negative opinions, their objectives will be met.
10. People will follow leadership when they understand what the leaders are offering and stay focused on their goals.

Promising Future

In our promising future, we all are going to encounter some clouds. These clouds are part of living. Clouds are needed to bring rain. I've never seen rain that comes from the clear blue sky. Have you? Clouds denote rain, storms and bad weather. The word of God tells us that there are other types of clouds that are just as destructive as the clouds that bring rain and storms. These are the clouds in our lives to test our faith, our willingness to follow God, and His teachings.

Clouds will slow you down. Clouds will make you think, *am I doing the right thing?* Clouds will make you stop in your tracks. Clouds will make you fall on your knees and cry out to God at midnight hours, and call on God for the right directions. Some clouds are so heavy and dark, and some are so black and fearful they just weigh you down and you just have to wait, and wait, pray and pray until the storms have passed over. One of the Great Hymns of the Church is "Stand By Me:"

> ***"Stand By Me"***
> When the storms of life are raging, stand by me;
> When the storms of life are raging stand by me;
> When the world is tossing me like a ship upon the sea;
> Thou who rulest wind and water, stand by me (stand by me)
> (The New Hymnal of the Christian Methodist Episcopal Church,
> Page 500)

The Bible says this is what happened to the children of Israel. When the clouds were so heavy and dark around the

PILLAR IV: The Community

tabernacle, Moses just had to wait on the Lord to remove the clouds of darkness and bring on the pillars of fire by night. Once God spoke and entered the Tabernacle they were able to move forward under the directions of the Almighty God.

In my opinion, there seems to be a historical parallel connection between the Israelites and Colored folks, Negros, Blacks and African Americans. We as a race of people have been caught in many clouds in our journey. Yet we have had a glorious past since leaving the Mother Land, with the signing of the Emancipation Proclamation 1863 and the Civil Rights Bills in 1965.

As I said before, we have come a mighty long way since those days of slavery, through hard times of the depression years, through the glory years of prosperity and the lean years of the recession. God has brought us through many clouds of the past and to where we are today.

In 1950, I had an opportunity to visit Tuskegee Institute. On the campus I saw Booker T. Washington's Monument, called "Lifting the Veil" standing at the center of the campus. The inscription at its base reads, "He lifted the veil of ignorance from his people and pointed the way to progress through education and industry." What was Booker T. Washington lifting? He was telling us to use our minds and hands. *Till the ground and become industrialized. Cast down your bucket where you are. Study, get a good education, and learn to use your hands and mind.*

In 1967 Mayor Richard Gordon Hatcher was elected mayor of Gary, Indiana and Mayor Carl Stokes was elected Mayor of Cleveland, Ohio. These two outstanding young Black leaders started a movement that broke the political power of white supremacy that was in control for more than 150 years. This controlling force refused to elect Black mayors and Blacks to

PILLAR IV: The Community

any major positions on city, county, state and national levels in the United States.

Under the leadership of Mayor Richard Gordon Hatcher, and many other Black leaders in 1972, called a Black Political Convention in Gary, IN to develop a Black Agenda that drew 8,000 attendees. Black leaders came together from across the country to address problems that faced people of color. The writer of this book was privileged to give the opening prayer at the Black Political Convention in 1972, and was privileged to give the closing prayer and benediction on Saturday August 29, 2015 at the Celebration of the 1972 National Black Political Convention: A New Generation of Leaders dinner at the Genesis Center. An electrifying speech was delivered by the son of the Co-founder of the 1972 National Black Political Convention. His father, The Honorable Baraka, gave the Key Note address.

Amira Baraka's son Ras Baraka, the 40th Mayor of Newark, New Jersey, made an astute observation about Black leaders and 21st Century politics. Mayor Baraka spoke of how royal foods or "King meat" as a metaphor that represents the corrupt financial perks that continue to jeopardize and destroy the careers of Black political leaders and the communities they serve. With unemployment and poverty still prevalent among Blacks in Gary and across the nation, Baraka urged leaders to defy themselves and instead go on a Daniel Fast, a religiously rooted, short-term eating plan drawn from the Book of Daniel, which appears in the Old Testament. "Our children are being bred and fed on the king's meat and you wonder why they are not doing well in school and in life", Baraka said. "We need to make our own food and our own recipes." (The Garry Crusader Volume LIV number 19-Saturday, September 5, 2015.)

PILLAR IV: The Community

Oh what a glorious past. When I look back to 2008 and witness when the first Black President was elected, President Obama. I saw the hands of God moving throughout America and the world. I had to jump out of my seat and thank God and shout "Glory, Glory. Thank you Jesus!!" When we think of our glorious past, we must think of our mothers and fathers. We must think of who they were, where they came from, and the glorious times when they were Colored, Negroes, Blacks and now African Americans.

History tells us we were unlike any other ethnic group; we were separated, disconnected, detached, disrupted, disengaged, disaffected, dehumanized, disappointed, and demoralized. We know less about our ancestors and have less respect for our fore fathers than any other ethnic group. African Americans or their descendants were enslaved and had no claim by birth or family or wealth or land or resources of any kind. They could not claim a family name. And yet they still prevailed and still impressed their children to get a good education.

When we were "Colored" we had bonding relationships in our communities with our churches, families, and schools. We knew people by name that lived in our communities. We had businesses; restaurants, hotels, banks, grocery stores, service stations, dry cleaners, laundromats, and recreational centers. We had pastors and professional people who lived in the communities. Pastors, school principals, teachers, business owners and politicians walked through the community and showed ownership, because they lived there.

Citizens who lived in the community and those who visited the community respected their leaders. Fathers were strong men active in the welfare of the lives of all of the people who lived in the community. It was a safe community. Churches and schools were in partnership in teaching and reaching the

PILLAR IV: The Community

needs of the children and the families. The schools and churches were meeting places. Look how our communities have changed in the last forty years.

The churches and the schools need to be in partnership more so today in order to resolve the critical needs of broken homes, students, teachers and parents. The lack of understanding of the school rules and regulations needed to help all students get a good education. We need churches as open centers for students to use as a safe haven until parents are off work, student tutoring, and counseling that will help them to find themselves regarding their future and their daily schedules.

Elected officials and appointed leaders who build their reputations on false pretenses, and quick gimmicks will soon fall in to their own trap. The public has an obligation to hold their leaders to high standards and accountability for the way they act and perform their duties. Demand they tell the truth and help them to overcome their weaknesses. Citizens have a Christian responsibility to pray for their leaders at all times for God to guide them in making wise decisions that are in the best interest of the people who elected them.

We see this before our nation and everywhere there are national leaders, religious leaders, political leaders, educational leaders, family leaders and those in other leadership positions, and all faiths need to repent before their God and the people for the sins they have committed. It has been said "you can fool some of the people some of the time, but you cannot fool all of the people all the time."

In today's world, citizens are more informed regarding the issues that are before them. This is true because of news through newspaper, radio, TV, social media and texting (the new word-of-mouth) and they are reporting news up to the minute on all subjects. There is no reason why the public should not be knowledgeable on current events of what is taking place in even some of the remote areas of the world. This information should enable the public to scrutinize, analyze and decipher information intelligently without been misled. In many communities there are group sessions that are organized to help the public to get a better understanding and become better informed on all issues that are before the nation.

The public should not be ignorant on subjects that are before the school board, city government, state government and government on the national level. It is your responsibility to be a voice in your schools, local, state and national governments. As parents and family members you owe it to your children and community to make your voices heard for changes that are needed to make progress and build stability.

The only way you can do this, you must use your voices and talents by supporting your institutions by making things better for your children and the needs of the people. You do this by making your voices heard in school board meetings, visiting your child's school and observing what is taking place at the school; in the classroom and on the playground. You need to know your child's teachers name, guidance counselor, principal and the curriculum that is offered in the school. When parents lose interest and show no concern, chances are the teachers and school administration will gradually lose interest in their children.

> "By day the Lord went ahead of them in a pillar of cloud to guide them on their way and by night in a pillar of fire to give them light, so that they could travel by day or night. Neither the pillar of cloud by day nor the pillar of fire by night left its place in front of the people." Exodus 13:21-22.

PILLAR IV: The Community

What has God given us so that we can have the same assurance? The Bible; something the Israelites did not have. Look to God's Word for reassurance of his presence. As the Hebrews looked to the pillars of cloud and fire, we can look to God's Word day and night to know he is with us, helping us on our journey. The pillars of fire and cloud were examples of theophany – God appearing in a physical form. In this form God lit Israel's path, protected them from their enemies, provided reassurance, controlled their movements, and inspired the burning zeal that Israel should have for their God. The greatness of a people can be achieved if God is allowed to lead.

1. Elected officials become accountable
2. Civil Rights Bills become the law of the land
3. All children enroll in school
4. Black Lives Matter

The Glory of God returned to the people in their leadership roles: religious leaders, civic leaders and key persons with know-how, to accomplish goals without giving up. When people are involved in their educational pursuit of mentoring, developing programs to broaden their scope of understanding relationships through workshops, love feasts, revivals, true confessions, powerful Bible studies, powerful preaching, teaching, worshipping, congregations, great music, powerful singing, members showing love toward each other, friendly attitudes toward visitors, strangers, sinners, homeless, rejects and all of the creations of God.

If these spiritual points are adhered to and taught in families, schools, churches, and communities, that will become driving forces that enable people to accomplish their goals of rebuilding family structures, financial goals, housing for its people, schools for its citizens, jobs, cities free of crimes,

PILLAR IV: The Community

good police and fire departments, and a strong business community that works for all of its citizens.

It has been said by some writers historically Black churches don't show enough concern for their people and especially in the communities where their churches are located. We daily see the activities that are taking place in our communities and only give lips service to what needs to be done. Each week, month and year the problems become out of control and the people become less interested in their churches and communities.

As a result too many of our children are dropping out of families, dropping out of schools, dropping out of Sunday schools, and dropping out of the communities. When dropouts occur they have no place to go to restore their character. Too many of the Black fathers, young males and boys are incarcerated. Black women and Black girls are having more problems finding a soul brother to relate to.

Too many parents, churches and faith based organizations are not supporting their schools and communities in their projects. It's time for churches and community leadership to raise the standard barrier for our children, standing on corners begging for money to help in their schools, churches and community projects to buy uniforms, band instruments, church projects. It sends a negative message to our children that they have to beg to get what they want. As pastors and community leaders, we must do a better job in teaching our people about stewardship.

Should there be a living presence in the community; is there a church within the context of the wild. Or has the church discarded the value of the marginalized? The artists of modern music seem to answer or reflect the lack of spiritual authority within our communities' best. Perhaps we should be listening with greater intent.

> **No Church in the Wild**
> *(Jay Z, Kanye West)*
> Human beings in a mob
> What's a mob to a king?
> What's a king to a god?
> What's a god to a non-believer?
> Who don't believe in anything?
> We make it out alive
> All right, all right
> No church in the wild
> Tears on the mausoleum floor
> Blood stains the Coliseum doors
> Lies on the lips of a priest
> Thanksgiving disguised as a feast
> Rollin' in the Rolls-Royce Corniche
> Only the doctors got this, I'm hidin' from police
> Cocaine seats
> All white like I got the whole thing bleached
> Drug dealer chic
> I'm wonderin' if a thug's prayers reach
> Is Pious pious 'cause God loves pious?
> Socrates asks, "whose bias do y'all seek?"
> All for Plato, screech
> I'm out chere' ballin', I know y'all hear my sneaks
> Jesus was a carpenter, Yeezy, laid beats
> Hova flow…

Our mission: to return to the Great Commission of Christ by any spiritual means necessary for survival sake.

PILLAR IV: The Community

Conclusion

For centuries, philosophers, scientists, economists, and great legal minds have theorized and debated over what should be considered the most important institution in society, and therefore the essential foundation of a good and healthy society. There are those who say that the government is the foundation of society, because government can make, enforce, and change laws. There are those who say that only the economy can be the true foundation for a good society, because the economy is what produces the goods and services which are needed by society. There are others who will promote the family, the community, or religious institutions as the one true core of a society.

Many years of reflection and praying while ministering to families, and communities, have opened my heart to see what God desires to be the soul and foundation of a healthy society. What God has revealed to me is the source and reason for the writing of this book, "The Four Pillars of Society." In God's eyes, a society does not have one essential foundation but four; the Family, the School, the Church, and the Community.

The Family, which was created by God when He made man and woman; "male and female created He them" (Genesis 1:27). "He blessed them, and God said unto them, be fruitful and multiply, and replenish the earth, and subdue it." (Genesis 1:28). The Family is the very first school the child will attend. It will be the parent who has the charge to keep for teaching the child right and wrong, even as he or she learns to walk and talk.

The Church is the place where the young and the old are taught essential moral and spiritual lessons. The Church teaches the true meaning of love, what it means to be in love and charity with your neighbors, and how to fear the God in whom all people move and have their being. Ultimately, the

PILLAR IV: The Community

Church has the charge of nurturing people towards finding eternal and abundant life through faith in Christ.

The School provides the space for not only learning the basics, but essential skills needed for work and for citizenship. School is where children learn how to make language, math, and science serve them. School is where critical thinking skills are developed, which will enable children to become mature and productive adults.

Community is the place where all individuals come together in their neighborhood, to live together, work together, and do business together. Community also serves as the place where the relationships which help form a more perfect union can be nurtured for the good of all.

I pray that the truths I learned, while writing this book, will also be learned by everyone who reads it. Society can only function in a dysfunctional way with only one foundation or Pillar, no matter how essential it may be. Our society will only be healthy, especially for our children, when the Four Pillars of Family, Church, School and Community are valued, protected, and preserved by all.

ACKNOWLEDGEMENTS

Many individuals have played a major role in my life, and have motivated me to stay focused on my journey in life.

First of all I must give tributes to my father and mother, Young Julius Cargle and Mariah Joanna Elliott Cargle for their Biblical teaching "Train Up a child in the way he should go; and when he is old, he will not depart from it" Proverbs 22:6.In this Christian foundation they laid for their twelve children. Their instructions and examples of living a Christian life helped and contributed to the foundations of my eleven (11) siblings Alice, Eula, Wallace, Gillie, Julius, Pedro, Josie, Frank, Sidney, Alma, Elmer, myself included and our spouses. Each of us continual to build on that foundation established by Jesus Christ, our parents, as we worship and fellowship with the saints at the Ebenezer C.M.E. Church, Hillsboro, Alabama. We all have kept the faith and prayed that our children will stay connected to the Body of Christ from generation to generation as they press on the upper way, to meet their beloved parents and relatives who have joined that great cloudy of witnesses.

God blessed me with the perfect wife in Belva June "Jean" Cargle. Although she is with the Lord, her legacy continues within the pages of this book, with our children, family and friends. I would like to acknowledge her constant love, support and direction throughout our marriage and my ministry. Belva was a phenomenal educator, community activist and First Lady. Through Belva's guidance and direction, we shared together our most valuable lesson...to do God's work in our family, the school, the Church and the community.

I thank God for my adult sons, Carrell, Jr. and Derrick, and my daughter Carla for their encouragements they have shared with on the various contents of this book. Also, I give thanks

Acknowledgements

to my niece Stephanie Buchanan for her suggestions. I thank God for Rev. Dr. Joseph B. Gordon, for his constructive advice. I must also thank my (Spiritual Son in the Ministry,) the Rev. Dr. David L. Bryant, Jr., for the time we shared together in our discussions of the content in my book.

After many hours of praying at my altar, asking God and Jesus Christ to direct the right person with the Christian touch, and writing skills to edit and eternalize the contents into a readable book that families, schools, churches and communities will enjoy reading and discussing in family gathering, workshops, classrooms, church leadership schools and community outreach sessions. I thank God for directing me to Rev. Judy C. Esco, a young lady I have known for many years. Her leadership skills and professional training became known as she participated in her local church and district as lead person for the District Evangelism Commission, as an associate pastor and leading pastor of a local church. Rev. Judy C. Esco was truly a God sent person for me to place hundreds of pages in her care to edit into readable chapters: 1. The Family, 2. The School, 3. The Church, 4. The Community. Also, Mrs. Rosie G. Washington for her skillful writing style in finalizing THE FOUR PILLARS OF SOCIETY for publication. To my niece, Wynter Lynn Ogele, for her artistic drawing of the initial The Four Pillars of Society.

Also, I would like to extend a special word of thanks to Mr. Jim Swanson for several motivating books and words of encouragement throughout this writing process.

I want to thank God for my spiritual son in Ministry, Bishop Henry M. Williamson, Sr., for agreeing to write the introduction. I wanted someone who knew me as a father, pastor, Presiding Elder and a community activist, who always wanted to make a difference in the lives of people in all walks of life.

Acknowledgements

I am grateful to Bishop Sylvester Williams, for agreeing to write the preface and expressions of thought. I shall never forget the leadership role that Rev. Dr. Sylvester Williams played in pulling a leadership team of committed workers in planning and executing one of the most outstanding and successful retirement celebrations held in my honor. This celebration drew a cross section of people from the local, connectional church, faith based, political and community outreach organizations.

I must express my appreciations to my father in ministry The Rev. W.H. Amos, (elected Bishop 1962) for his guiding counsel and the Rev. William H. Graves, Sr. (elected Bishop 1982) when we both were local Preachers under the guiding hand of Rev. Amos, we both learned how to relate to our bishops, presiding elders, ministers and laity.

I thank God for all of the bishops that thought enough of me to appoint me as one of their pastors and a member of their leadership team. Bishop J. Claude Allen, my first Bishop, thought enough of me and saw leadership skills, commitment, dedication and love for the C.M.E. Church, and ordained me to the Office of Deacon on September 19, 1959, and also ordained me to the Officer of Elder, September 20, 1959 at Grace C.M.E Church, Detroit, Michigan and admitted me into Full Connection at the close of the Annual Conference on Sunday, September 20, 1959. At the close of the South East, Missouri, Illinois, Wisconsin Conference, I was assigned to the Holsey Temple C.M.E. Church, St Joseph, Mo., in October, 1959.

I am grateful to God to have been blessed to serve under some of the most gifted and spiritual theologians and preachers. Each of them exhibited par excellence in their administrative leadership roles. These are the listing of bishops according to the status of my serve. Bishop J. Claude

Acknowledgements

Allen, Bishop Bertram W. Doyle, Bishop J. Claude Allen, Bishop W.H. Amos, Bishop Henry C. Bunton, Bishop Elisha P. Murchison, Bishop C. A. Kirkendoll and Bishop Dotcy I. Isom, Jr. My friendship with Bishop Isom began at Grace C.M.E. Church, Detroit, MI and continued after his election to the Episcopacy. He appointed of me as Pastor of the Israel CME Church and promoted me as the Presiding Elder on the Gary and Chicago Districts. I am also grateful for the leadership of Bishop Paul A. G. Stewart, Sr. and Bishop Sylvester Williams, Sr. All of these fathers have contributed much in their tenure of supervision over the Third Episcopal District.

Appendix

Reflecting back to traveling 276 miles round trip from Champaign, Illinois to the South Side of Chicago, Illinois every month in the heat, sleet, rain and snow to attend one of the Presiding Elder, Rev. Carrell K. Cargle Sr., monthly 2nd Sunday ministers training meeting for the Chicago district. The meetings would take place at Calvary CME Church, a little white church on the corner, at 1356 West 110th Street in Chicago, Illinois. Every meeting would open with a prayer in the basement of the church, and continental breakfast for those future leaders who would arrive early before the training. The host Pastor, Willie May Tyus of Calvary CME Church on the Southside of Chicago, was uplifting and would always be willing to speak life and vision to the young exhorters, local preachers, deacons and elder's ears.

The meeting was very instructional and uplifting. They would give young ministers a platform to learn the history of Methodism, the movement in the CME church's history from being known as Colored Methodist to Christian Methodist by the founding fathers. The Elders meeting was inspiring to those who had a desire to learn and develop their God given gifts to express their calling before the people without troubling the local pastor about getting practical opportunities. The Elder's meeting gave the ministers in attendance the opportunity to understand from a practical standpoint the meaning and purpose of different types of prayers, such as understanding the difference between a Pastoral prayer and an Invocation prayer. They would gain instructions on how to develop segments of a Methodist style of order of service. Each preacher was given the opportunity to draft a mock order of worship service, then execute the order of service during the training before the Elder and seasoned pastors who were also a part of the minister examination committee of the annual conference. On the 2nd Saturday of every month, ministers in training were given the chance to lead a local congregation in songs from the Methodist Hymnal.

Last but not least, the Elder's training gave each preacher an opportunity to proclaim the gospel in front of other ministers in training. Next, they were placed on a platform before experienced Pastors within the district to share wisdom from their personal experiences from within their local parishes. This would help the younger ministers learn from their mistakes and profit from their success. The Elder's training over a 4 to 5 year span prepared me to worship, lead, witness, and develop sound theology, Christology, history pertaining to Methodism. It also helped to handle particular meetings in the CME context and develop personally to represent God and His church before people. Thank you Elder Cargle for your vision, insight, and wisdom to develop preachers from the "little white church house" on the South Side of Chicago, Illinois to move preachers across the district and the church at

Appendix

large to become church planters, Pastors, Presiding Elders, and Presiding Prelates. Your prayers, instructions, wise council, and hard work for God and the church have not gone in vain. May God continue to bless you, your family, and ministry, now and for evermore!

Pastor/Founder: Rev. Byron L. Smith, Sr., M.Div., M.A. Clinical Psychology
Lifting The Veil Ministries Carson, CA.
www.liftingtheveiltosee.com

The following persons accepted the Call to Christian Services under the leadership of Pastor Cargle. Also, during his leadership as Presiding Elder of Gary and Chicago Districts of the Christian Methodist Episcopal Church people continue to serve. Several have and/or continue to serve as pastors or other administrative capacities.

Sons in Ministries

Rev. Henry M. Williamson, Sr.	Rev. Steven Deloney
Rev. David L. Bryant, Jr.	Rev. Cecil D. Beatty*
Rev. Carrell K. Cargle, Jr.	Rev. Donald Goosby*

Presiding Elder Leadership

Bishop Henry M Williamson, Sr.	Rev. Charles Coleman
Bishop Sylvester Williams, Sr.	Rev. Gregory Clemmons
Bishop Marvin F. Thomas, Sr.	Rev. Berdia Moffet
Bishop Lance Davis	Rev. Cecil Watson
Rev. Dr. Phillip D. Washington, P. E.	Rev. Lurline Clay
Rev. Dr. O'Nell Shyne, Jr.	Exhorter Jason Taylor
Rev. Dr. Essie Clark-George	Rev. Etta Maria Hadnot
Rev. Dr. Patricia Havis, P.E.	Minister Kila Johnson
Rev. Karen Walker-McClure, P.E,	Rev. Marcus J. Rogers
Rev. Tracey Jackson, P.E.	Rev. Stephanie Bradley
Rev. James Hendricks, Sr. PE	Minister Phillip March
Rev. Carrell K. Cargle, Jr.	Minister Clifton Hill
Rev. David L. Bryant, Jr.	Exhorter Daniel Hoskins
Rev. Steven Deloney	Rev. Willie J Tyus
Rev. Cecil Beatty	Rev. J. Michael Wright
Rev. Dr. Charlie Haymes	Rev. Jeanette Harbin
Rev. Silas James, Jr.	Rev. David L Carde
Rev. W.J. G. Mc Lin, Sr.	Rev. Dr. Julius C. Clay
Rev Van Carl Williams	Rev. Joe Lewis Farrar*
Exhorter George Williams	Rev. Dr. Nichols l. Betts
Minister Doris Rogers	Rev. Dr. Claudia Robinson-Dunlap
Rev. Evelyn Darling*	Rev. Curtis Dunlap
Rev. Mittie Collier	Rev. Joseph Bouknight, Sr.

Appendix

Rev. Brenda L Lewis
Rev. Dr. Jessie Douglas, Sr.
Rev. Judy C Esco
Rev. Dernell Kress-Stams
Rev. Jerome Wheat
Rev. Antoinette Y Moody
Minister Samantha Woods
Minister Charlotte Woods
Rev. Joyce Dorch
Rev. Spencer jones
Rev. Terry Wheat
Rev. Dr. Barbara Deloney
Exhorter Mary Rudy
Rev. Pamela Bonds
Rev. Gertrude Franklin
Minister Francis Haggins
Rev. Rodney Montgomery
Rev. Gwendolyn Tolbert
Rev. Sandra Killian
Rev. Kimberly Beal
Rev. Alice Barr*
Rev. Stanley Hill
Rev. Roland brown
Rev. Jacqueline Mc Cowen
Rev. Brenda Johnson
Rev. Willie Nash, IV
Rev. Reginald T. Burke
Rev. Richard D. Shaw

Rev. Bryon Smith
Rev. Lavisha Walls-Williams
Rev. Willie B. Weaver
Rev. Cassandra Lynn Weaver
Rev. Harold L. Harrington, Sr. *
Rev. Carmen G. Williams
Rev. John C. Clemons
Rev. Nathaniel Smiley
Rev. Cornelius Harper
Rev. Cletonia Harper
Rev. Larry Ellis
Minister Jell Jackson
Rev. Monte Williams
Minister Veronica Collier
Rev. Harold Edmonson, Jr.
Rev. Pamela Harrell
Rev. Henrietta Muse
Rev. Frank Nesbitt
Rev. Danie Johnson
Rev. Julio Andujo
Rev. Felicia Campbell
Rev. Charles H. Shyne, Jr *
Rev. Derrick Price
Rev. Dr. Jerome B. Price, Sr *
Rev. Dr. Jessie L. Douglas, Sr.
Rev. Andrea Gardner
Rev. Mark Tribble

Denotations
*Deceased
P.E. Presiding Elder

Moving Forward to Show "Black Life Matters"... and More
A Report to the CME Church on Subsequent Request from Three Senior Bishops
By Senior Bishop Lawrence Reddick, CME Church

The three Senior Bishops of the African Methodist Episcopal Church {AME}, African Methodist Episcopal Zion, {AME Zion} and Christian Methodist Episcopal {CME} Churches met with others on December 19th in Charlotte, N.C., to confer on strategies for what we emphasized to you in December a "Black Life Matters" campaign.

Appendix

On December 19th the three Senior Bishops [Bishop John R. Bryant, AME; Bishop George E. Battle, Jr., AME Zion; and Bishop Lawrence Reddick, {CME} were joined by these other representatives of our denominations: Rev. Vincent Andujo, St Louis, Mo. {CME}; Rev. James Bailey, Chicago, ILL. {AME}, Rev. Jamal Harrison Bryant, Baltimore, Md. {AME}; Mr. Kenneth Dunston, Raleigh, N.C. {AME Zion}; Rev. Gregory King, Alexandria, Va.[CME] ; Rev. Dr. Staccato Powell, Raleigh, N.C. {AME Zion}; Rev. Shazetta Thompson-Hill, Medon, Tenn. {CME}; and Mr. Herb Watkins, Charlotte, N.C. {AME Zion} . Also present was Bishop Leonard Bolick, Bishop of North Carolina for the Evangelic Lutheran Church in America. We met at the AME Zion Church Headquarters.

The Three Senior Bishops and their Leadership teams agreed to put forward to their denominational groups:
1) We as your Senior Bishops intend to make our presence felt in Ferguson, Missouri, and to do something specific while there to support the dreams of people like Michael Brown and his family To do so, these are the agreements we came to:
   a. We agreed to go as Senior Bishops to Normandy, Missouri (another St. Louis suburb where Michael Brown's Ferguson neighbors go to public high school), on Monday, January 12, 2015.
   b. We agreed to seek at least three scholarships- one representing each of our constituencies from one of the Colleges traditionally associated or affiliated with the AME, AME Zion, and CME Churches. As your Senior Bishop, I have conferred or asked to confer with the chairs of the Boards of Trustees and the Presidents of these Colleges about ways we as CMEs can help to sponsor such scholarships. We understand that if this College (s) agrees participate in this offering, the terms and guidelines of title scholarship offers shall be guided by the Colleges' administrations.
   c. We agreed to ask our Youth Presidents (in the CME case will be our Young Adult President, Reverend Keenan Winters) to go with us to the Normandy school on January 12, 2015 with the request that they speak to the assembly with the announcement, while the three Senior Bishops stand solidarity with our respective presidents.
   d. We also agreed to make ourselves available on that day [persons who wish to speak concerns to us; and, furthermore, make ourselves available for future expressions to us through social media.
2) Knowing that there is a need for authentic action beyond the symbolic witness was shared within the walls of our congregation on December 14th. We are asking our congregations to make a presence

felt in the many communities where we are planted around by moving out of the churches on the Sundays of the Dr. Martin Luther King, Jr., Holiday-Sunday, January 1, 2015- following morning worship.
   a. Thus, we are asking you to move beyond the symbol of black" within the walls of our churches and do a "Walk Out from all of our churches into our communities on Sunday, January 18, following the morning worship. If you are located in a town or city where you count "blocks"- please walk at least six blocks in your neighborhood to show you care and concern. If there are people in your neighborhood who do not know you, please introduce yourself and become acquainted along the way.
   b. If you are located in a rural area where the next house is a long way from the worship place, please intention about moving within a radius of 3 to 6 miles to show you are concerned for who is in your neighborhood and to let them know you are representatives of God's Church in the community.
   c. And remember: our objective for the Walk Out is to make the presence of the churches known in every community around the nation, with the understanding that (as some said), "there is a Ferguson in every community." Let us walk out to symbolize the unity of mutual support and strengthening that comes through building relationships understanding.
3) Based upon our agreement in conversation on December 15 that one of the primary underpinnings of success in America is growth in economics, we agreed to work together for an economic impact day- specifically, April 4, 2015 (which is the anniversary of Dr. King's death as well as the day before Easter)-or ask all of our people members to effactually show the impact of Black economics in our communities by buying nothing on that day except those items available through Black entrepreneurs.

We cannot let the serious needs and tragedies of the past months go by without our active involvement for justice. We believe the three requests we are making are creative and helpful. We will come together again in the near future, and we will continue to work together toward justice and healing in our nation.

The mantra began, "Black lives matter." It is still true. But as witness the carelessness with which lives have been taken, the predominance of violence in our communities, and as we witness the precious little thought given to persons of all races when it comes to the callous ways lives are ended in violence, we have to remembers that the statements are also true: Brown life matters. Yellow life matters. Black life matters. White life

Appendix

matters. Yes, ALL LIFE MATTERS, for God made from one flesh all of people of the world. (Source ref: Bishop Lawrence L. Reddick III)

The National Civil Rights Hall of Fame
(Insert taken from the 50th Anniversary program booklet in celebration of the Honorable Richard Gordon Hatcher, the First Black Mayor in the United States of America: November 4, 2017)

Mayor Richard Gordon Hatcher
1967 – 1987

The American Civil Rights Movement is responsible for state, local and national laws and court decisions which mandate fair treatment and equal opportunity in public accommodations, employment, voting, housing and education. This movement continues to open doors and makes it possible for people of color, women, older Americans and the disabled to move into widespread areas of the American society. Many of the artifacts, documents and memorabilia associated with and depicting this great sweep of American history are in danger of being lost, destroyed or discarded with each passing day, thus the National Civil Rights Hall of Fame is created to preserve and promote this rich historical legacy for future generations. The campaign to build the National Civil Rights Hall of Fame in Gary, Indiana began many years ago under the esteemed leadership of Bishop Andrew Grutka of the Gary Diocese, and the renowned educator, H. Theodore Tatum, Principal of Roosevelt High School. Both of these great citizens of the region have passed on, however, many others continue the effort to finish their work.

The National Civil Rights Hall of Fame will provide America with a highly visible focal point where adults and all of the Nation's children, black, white, and all shades in between, can learn of the sacrifices made to open the doors of opportunity for all citizens of the United States. The project will be located in the State of Indiana, Northwest Indiana region, in the City of Gary, Indiana. Gary is a city in Lake County, Indiana 25 miles from downtown Chicago, Illinois. It is adjacent to the Indiana Dunes Lakeshore and borders Lake Michigan. The city is known for having elected one of the first African American Mayors in the country, namely, Richard Gordon Hatcher, its large steel mills, and for being the birthplace of Michael Jackson and the Jackson5 music entertainment group.

The facility will contain cutting edge technology, such as a holographic representation, laser presentations, and extensive use of the worldwide web to expand the scope of exhibits on display. The National Civil Rights Hall of Fame will also contain a research library where many of the important documents related to the Movement will be preserved and made available to scholars, researchers, and students. It will bring visitors to and create economic benefits for the city of Gary, Lake and Porter Counties and the State of Indiana during both the construction phase of the project and resulting from ongoing operations.

Upon completion, the NATIONAL CIVIL RIGHTS HALL OF FAME will be a state of art facility. The historic Hall of Fame will rekindle a spirit of pride, promote a sense of community and unity, increase levels of affection and regard for our city, and serve as a living monument to the rich and glorious history and contributions of people who have been a part of this struggle.

The estimated cost for the project is $14,000,000. As we again aggressively pursue funding from our city, state, and federal governments, most recently through the city of Gary and Mayor Karen Freeman-Wilson, the National Civil Rights Hall of Fame received a $59,500 grant for a feasibility study from the U.S. Economic Development Administration. To date, our local fundraising efforts have brought in close to $500,000 and we are continuing these efforts. Our goal is to make the National Civil Rights Hall of Fame a reality.

We're looking forward to our groundbreaking and completion of this project, and want you to be a part of this effort through your participation in our membership drive. Our planned construction date is January 1, 2019.

National Civil Rights Institute & Hall of Fame Board Executive Committee
Richard G, Hatcher, Founder & President
Lamar Taylor, Board Member & Executive Committee Chairman

What an attraction they all will bring to Gary, Northwest Indiana, Chicago and the Mid-West, as they travel east and west, north and south on Interstates Highways 94, 80,294, 280, 65, 57, 55 and toll road I-90, also by Air Gary /Chicago Metropolitan Airport. What an attraction that will become when community leaders connecting people together use their resources and expertise to market this area and have it become a financial jewel. To see thousands of people are hired and billions of dollars flowing into the economy through tourism. What an opportunity for residents to witness the need to build hotels, restaurants, and have vendors available to accommodate tourists coming to enjoy Michael Jackson & Jackson Five Museum.

The hope was that the museum would connect all parks as people travel east and west, north and south. What a bright future, when bankers, investiture, politicians, pastors, faith based organizations, educators, families, and community leaders, working together to achieve workable goals that are profitable for all!

All goals and visions can become reachable when all of the major players, financial institutions, personalities, and families come together on the same page working faithfully until the goals have been accomplished. All things are possible when families, schools, leadership teams, churches and community unite their efforts by coming uniting together to make all things possible for the good of people of all faiths.

Legacy Connections
Parents have been given the authority by God "To train up a child in the way he should go; And when he is old, he will not depart from it." Proverbs 22:6 *(KJ SB)*

Parental training will help a child develop a taste for things of God. The home is a preparatory school for life, a culture center understanding of quietness, peace, love, gentle touch of filling that established contact with the mother and father as the child develops mentally, spiritually and physically each day to become healthy by parents who are praying for their child to become a gifted child as it grows and observe what is taking place in his room and surrounding.

Dr. James Comer of the Yale University Child Study Center launched his School Development Program (SDP) and stressed the need for parental involvement and building true partnerships of trust between the school staff and parents. In fact, constructive and neighborhood schools began to lose their identities, when families began to move out of their neighborhoods into new areas of the city, suburban, and town searching for better homes, schools and better communities to raise their families.

This created an opportunity for many of the professional families to exit from their communities and schools. As families were leaving their homes many of the white populations had already left the neighborhoods and city. That created some of the crises in the first place, because they did not want their children attending schools where the academic levels were decreasing and crimes in the schools were increasing and less learning was taking place.

Some writers have stated academic achievements in the last fifty or sixty years began to decline when integration and desegregation became the law for public housing and schools. Whites immediately started searching for better towns and cities, to move their families and enrolled their children in better schools in those communities. They were relocating. As a result of desegregation, many Blacks left their predominately black neighborhoods and moved to integrated neighborhood within the cities, suburban areas and townships.

This created a mass exit which caused many cities to lose populations, tax bases, businesses left cities, and no jobs, many of the neighborhoods schools closed and were boarded up. Many of the family homes were anchors in the community and show cases where professional, stake holder and business people once lived. Those properties are now boarded up and what once was the show place of striving schools that graduated outstanding students, who excelled in sports, education, science, arts, lawyer, medical doctor, politicians and math are now leaders, and CEOs in their profession and in major companies, institutions across the world.

In their communities where they once walked the streets to and from their schools, and churches where they were educated, received their Christian training, baptized, and married. And the beautiful homes where they once lived have now become fields of grass, and weeds that have over grown boarded up homes, schools, parks and businesses.
What was once the cultural center of their neighborhoods, have now become a cancer to all of the people who once lived there and those who reside there.

The Midwest has something to shout about! Let's take a look where we are today in 2015, look back over one hundred years and see some of the major historical developmental sites that stand as a monument for the future connecting the future with the past. The past we see Indiana Dunes, Marquette Park, Gary, IN, the Steel Capital of the World, the Old Pullman Neighborhood that built Pullman cars on the south end of Chicago, where President Barack Obama has designated the Pullman Neighborhood as a National Historic District and National Park. The President's Committees selected President Barack Obama's Library to be built on the Southside of Chicago, near the University of Chicago in one of the parks known as Jackson or Washington Park.

Appendix

Gary, Indiana Steel Capital of the World attracted immigrants from all over the world, and from the states of Alabama, Mississippi, Arkansas, and Georgia, seeking jobs to better their living conditions. Today we look to the future and see the building of a Michael Jackson, and The Jackson Five Entertainment Arts Museum Complex in Gary, where thousands of travelers visit 2300 Jackson Street each year just to see their birth place.

REFERENCES

- Life Application Bible, New International Version, Tyndale Publishers, Inc.
- Matthew Henry Commentary
- King James Bible, Study Edison
- Genesis: An Expositional Commentary, Volume 1, Genesis 1:1-11, 32, James Montgomery Boice
- Webster's New World Dictionary of The American Language
- Achievement Matters, Hugh B. Price 2002, Kensington Publishing Corp., 2002
- Allan Boesak, Black and Reformed, 1984 Orbis Books
- And Are We Yet Alive by Richard B. Wike, Abingdon Press, Nashville
- Leadership Is The Key: Unlocking Your Ministry Effectiveness by Herb Miller, Abingdon Press
- CME Pocket Ritual Page 68: by Bishop Marshall Gilmore, Editor
- The Book of Discipline of The Christian Methodist Episcopal Church, Published by CME Church
- Half Black Half White by Eugene Brooks, 2009
- Getting the Love You Want: A Guide For Couples, Harville Hendrix, Ph.D. 1988, Harper Perennial
- You, Family and God by Clifford Davis, Moody Press, 1957
- Reclaiming The Urban Family by Dr. Willie Richardson, Zondervan Publishing House
- Financial Truth: Your Mind + Your Mouth = Your Money by Carla J. Cargle, WBPH 2008
- Divorced... By Surprise by Rosezine B. Wallace, Xulon Press
- Healing Words, by Larry Dossey, M.D., Harper Press, San Francisco
- Teaching Our Faith In God, by L. Harold DeWolf, Abingdon Press 1963
- Strengthening Families and Communities 2009 Resource Guide, Dept. of Health & Health Services
- Strengthening Families and Communities 2010 Resource Guide, Dept. of Health & Health Services
- Pre Martial Counseling Techniques and Their Theological Significance by Carrell K. Cargle, Sr. 1967
- Moving forward to Show "Black Life Matters" and More: A Report to the CME Church on Subsequent Request from Three Senior Bishops, by Senior Bishop Lawrence Reddick, III, December 31, 22014
- Affordable Care Act, The Black Star Project, 2014
- Healthy Families and Children Dropout Prevention

References

- Let's Listen: Group Discussion With Out – Of - School Youth, Gary, In., October 10, 2008
- Work One: Northwest Indiana Workforce Board, Inc., Gary Education Leadership Council
- The Times, Hometown Thriller: Family Talks about Michael, Plans for a Museum, August 27, 2011
- The Times, The Gary/Chicago International Airport Take Off, August 2015
- The Times, President: "Pullman is a Milestone in Our Journey", February 20, 2015
- The Gary Crusader, The National Civil Rights Hall of Fame Inspires Gary to Hope, Saturday, September 5, 2015
- The Chicago District Of The CME Church, Directory of Leaders 2002 – 2003, Ministry Beyond The Wall, by Dr. Carmichael Crutchfield
- Interfaith Prayer Power Pool, 37th Anniversary, Israel CME Church, Gary, In, November 7, 2015

These **protective factors** are critical for all parents and caregivers, regardless of the child's age, sex, ethnicity or racial heritage, economic status, special needs, or whether he or she is raised by a single, married or divorced parent or other caregivers. All of these factors work together to reinforce each other. For example, parents are more likely to be resilient in times of stress when they have social connections and a strong attachment to their child. Protective factors can provide a helpful conceptual framework for providers working with children and their families. (Source: Strengthening Families and Communities 2010 Resource page 10 Promoting Safe, Stable and Nurturing Relationships).

ABBREVIATIONS

AB	*Application Bible*
LAB	*Life Application Bible*
CME	*Christian Methodist Episcopal*
KJSB	*King James Study Bible*
NKJSB	*New King James Study Bible*
NKJB	*New King James Bible*
KJV	*King James Version*
NKJV	*New King James Version*
NIV	*New International Version*

###

Four Pillars of Society